IT'S YOUR DAY

IT'S YOUR DAY

WIL SHORB

Nashville
New York
ABINGDON PRESS

IT'S YOUR DAY

Copyright © 1973 by Abingdon Press

Library of Congress Cataloging in Publication Data

SHORB, WIL, 1938-   It's your day. Bibliography: p.
1. Meditations. I. Title.
BV4832.2.S522   242'.4   73-5778

ISBN 0-687-19764-3

Scripture quotations noted as follows:
JB—from The Jerusalem Bible, copyright © 1966 by Darton,
   Longman & Todd, Ltd. and Doubleday & Company, Inc.
   Used by permission of the publisher.
KJV—from the King James Version.
LB—from The Living Bible, copyright © 1971 by Tyndale
   House Publishers.
NBV—from The New Berkeley Version, copyright 1945, 1959,
   © 1969 by The Zondervan Publishing House.

MANUFACTURED BY THE PARTHENON PRESS AT
NASHVILLE, TENNESSEE, UNITED STATES OF AMERICA

TO MUZZ AND DID
with love

CONTENTS

When he pours his new life into the soul,
A new people he will surely make;
Only then can you drink the wine of life
If you'll make it happen—It's Your Day.
It's Your Day, *then live it, children;*
It has only begun to be;
Your day, God made it, said it,
"Come, spend your day with me."
             —from "It's Your Day" by Merl Shorb

Tonight, as I write these lines to you, I am thinking back. Back to where I was exactly one year ago. You see, it's that time of year again. Hail to the old. Cheers for the new.

The Shorb Brothers (Merl, Happy, and myself) were singing the old year out in a Washington, D.C., area restaurant. The man with the roving mike (remember him?) stopped by our table between performances and announced, "And, Wil Shorb, what do you think of New Year's resolutions, if I may ask?" My reply was casual: "I don't make 'em. New Year's resolutions aren't realistic. It's new day's resolutions that get results."

And that's the whole idea of the pages that follow. Life is made up of days. Not years. Not months. Not even weeks (or weekends!). Those are just ways of combining days. When we get it down to just days and start taking one at a time, changes begin to emerge in our life-styles—some quite remarkable.

It's uncanny, too, how the most unlikely individuals seem to succeed in this business of making each day count.

9

Some are people the world labels "uneducated," whatever that means. And vice versa. For there are Ph.Ds walking around who would come up what I will call *IV-F on life*. Unfortunately, they have never learned to handle:

1. their *failures* (no working philosophy of adversity)
2. their *feelings* (no control of temperament)
3. their *fatigue* (zero physical conditioning)
4. their so-called *freedoms*

I'll go back and explain who the Shorb Brothers are. We are what the name implies—three brothers named Shorb. We sing professionally—mostly at churches, colleges, and in public school assemblies. Pop music with a message. And what's the message? Well, it's all right here in these forty meditations—a collection of thoughts I have shared with audiences across America and Canada.

So—welcome to a Shorb Brothers concert without the music! And don't forget—*it's your day!*

OUR FAILURES

1
1,330 STRIKEOUTS

Aristotle said, "Learning is accompanied by pain."
Too many people won't go through that pain.
            —from *Your Key to Creative Thinking*
                by Robert Hutchins

The word *failure* immediately brings to mind the subject
of grades and school. But whereas only a few of us experience failure on report cards, all of us must confront
problems and setbacks in some area of our lives. In fact,
you tell people a lot about yourself by the manner in
which you react to adversity.

Take a sport like baseball. A man fails seven times out
of ten, and what do we call him? A loser? Hardly. He's
hitting .300 and is known as a superstar. Even though 70
percent of the time he doesn't "make it happen."

Every baseball fan knows that Babe Ruth hit 714 home
runs for an all-time record. But there is another record in
the books that few people are aware of. Babe Ruth struck
out 1,330 times. And that record has never been equaled
either.

The problem is that when successful people tell their
story, they usually paint a too-perfect picture. Very few
there are, candid enough to stand before an audience and
share failures and reverses (unless, of course, it fits neatly
into the total success image!). How often do you hear a
successful person tell of a setback that occurred, say, ten
years ago that they still don't understand? And yet, this
is the experience of everyone who reads this book, great
or small. This is life. Let's start telling it like it was!

It is so easy to overplay the game of life. On your first attempt at something, you shouldn't even be thinking of overall success or failure. This leads to discouragement. No one is at the top in every phase of his life. Did you know that Richard Nixon was a second-string tackle for most of four football seasons at Whittier College? Imagine —the future president of the United States cheering from the bench!

Victories will come, but almost never on the first try. After all, a little logic reveals that all that matters is eventual victory, no matter how many failures precede that victory. Right?

Thomas Edison plowed through ten thousand failures, but finally produced the electric lamp. Albert Einstein confessed to the world that he had been wrong in his conclusions 99 percent of the time. We hail their genius— but what about their philosophy of failure?

David in the Old Testament and Judas in the New are two Bible characters who each failed miserably. But there the similarity ends. David turned to God—"Have mercy upon me, O God" (Psalm 51:1 KJV)—Judas turned on himself and took his own life.

It is at the point of failure that we all have a chance to shine. It was in Peter's moment of failure on the Sea of Galilee that Jesus commanded him to "launch out into the deep" (Luke 5:4 KJV). Even as you read this (and as I write it), God may be trying to speak to us through a time when "we have toiled all the night, and have taken nothing." The frustration, the loneliness, the emptiness, can be turned into an opportunity.

When you encounter misfortune, think of someone you didn't like on first meeting, who later became your dearest friend. Just like making lemons into lemonade. Make this a habit. Work at it. Cultivate it. It must constantly be relearned.

Finally, some good advice from the Preacher (Ecclesiastes 11:6 JB): "In the morning sow your seed, do not let your hands lie idle in the evening. For which will prove successful, this or that, you cannot tell; and it may be that both will turn out well together." In other words, keep trying! Keep plugging away! Who can tell what will succeed and what won't?

If you don't achieve your goals in life, your failures or strikeouts won't be the reason. More likely it will be due to a lack of exposure or not enough effort. For perfectionism is unreal. When you go first-class, there are going to be strikeouts. If you're afraid of strikeouts, there aren't likely to be any home runs. It's as simple as that.

Learn a lesson from baseball this week. Try ten things for God. And if you are successful three times, guess what? You're a superstar, hitting an even .300!

2
THE GRATEFUL DEAD

Some men die in battle,
Some men die in flames,
But most men perish inch by inch
While playing little games.

Success is always very difficult to define. And it follows that failure is, too. I feel very strongly that true success is an extremely private affair. Because many of us see no "rewards" for our efforts, we mistakenly conclude that we have failed.

So often the quest for *status* gets in the way. And that is too bad. There is a current rock group called The Grateful Dead. In a sense, none of us ever find true life until we drop out, until we join the "grateful dead."

Billy Graham, in response to a newsman's question about his popularity, said, "Ever heard of Palm Sunday? That donkey Jesus was riding could have really had the big head. 'Boy, look at the crowd, listen to the cheers, they're even throwing down palm branches for me to walk on. I'm really something!' The donkey would have been completely in error. The crowd came to see Jesus. *I am like that donkey.* I am a conveyor of Jesus. The crowds come because they are hungry for God."

Jehovah reminded Ezekiel during a vision, "Pay attention to everything I show you, since you have only been brought here for me to show it to you" (Ezekiel 40:4 JB). Being used by God is not an ego trip. We have "only been brought here" to receive a message and pass it on to the people.

Too many times, the same Christian who abhors "approval-holism" in the world will immediately embark on the stereotyped voyage through the maze of religious or evangelical significance. Now the status game simply has a new ball park. But the game itself looks disturbingly familiar.

Grandpa Cilley was a Free Methodist preacher in the Adirondack Mountains of New York. Now my grandfather didn't exactly set the world on fire. Most he ever made was twenty dollars a week. His last church had two members. Two members. And one of those was Grandma!

Reminds me of an evangelistic tour Jesus once booked. Several boats sailed clear across the Sea of Galilee, through a violent storm. They reached, and delivered, *one person* who needed help. And with that mission accomplished, they all returned to the other side of the lake. How many of us would consider an endeavor of this nature successful? When we see one individual as the most important thing in the world, we are closer to Jesus' teaching on successful service.

As time goes by, I am impressed less and less by the spectacular. I'm sure God uses the spectacular—that isn't it. But as Adela Rogers St. Johns says in *Tell No Man*, "It might be easier to organize and impress a thousand people than to serve or heal one. Activity at any level sometimes covers a lot of emptiness." It gets to the point where religion can't make the news unless it is 2,300 of this or 500 of that. And this is misleading. Because what is really making this world tick, and where the real excitement is in Christianity, is found on the individual level— ordinary people who are faithful where they are, at home, at school, at work. *And that includes people who stand before large crowds on platforms.* They too will find their most effective witness in faithfulness to Jesus in the ordinary events of the day. It's got to start there, or it doesn't happen at all.

And there are no shortcuts. We align ourselves with a certain religious group, or philosophy, or set of standards, and think this immediately makes us part of the "in" group. In a word, spiritual. (Isn't it strange how efficiency in reciting and performing religious exercises so often becomes a thermometer for spiritual growth?) But it's just not that easy! Spiritual growth is a day-to-day thing, and slogans and clichés have little to do with it.

When Jesus spoke of deeds of spiritual significance, he mentioned giving someone a cold drink of water, feeding a hungry person, visiting a friend who is sick. And even in the midst of the crowd, Jesus demonstrated a sensitivity to the individual when he asked who had touched him.

The "professional" is found among the unemployed in the true kingdom of God. With heart and soul I believe that when God's voice finally begins to get through to us, we will be amazed at the seemingly menial tasks he is interested in. Write that letter. Visit so-and-so. Clean out the garage. And it's when we get into this area of insignificant obedience that we begin to discover where the real conflict is, and where the real battle is going on.

In the eleventh chapter of Genesis (verse 4 JB), a group of people (preparing to build the Tower of Babel) announce, "Let us make a name for ourselves." Contrast this with the very next chapter (12:2 JB), in which God says to Abraham, "I will bless you and make your name so famous that it will be used as a blessing." The godly man does not make a name for himself. This can only legitimately be an act of God. And I'll add that God sets the conditions. Abraham had to leave country, family, and heritage behind.

Here in the Washington area, we have the tomb of the Unknown Soldier. But if you look closely, you'll see it doesn't say an unknown soldier. The inscription reads, "Known but to God." And God does have his secrets.

Only he knows where Moses is buried. And to this day, Mozart's remains are in an unknown place—probably a pauper's grave in Vienna, they say. But God knows. Maybe he's the only one that needs to know.

Refocus your vision. Obsession with "success" can get you off the track. And God might have a better idea.

3
RESENTMENT

A visitor was watching his old friend plow. "I don't want to butt in," he said, "but you could save yourself a lot of work by saying 'gee' and 'haw' to that mule instead of just tugging on the lines." The old-timer mopped his brow. "Yep, I know that. But this mule kicked me six years ago and I ain't spoken to him since," he replied.

The most self-destructive reaction by far to things going wrong, to failure, is resentment. This baby is a real live killer. The word itself simply means "to re-sense" or "to relive." We all get hurt. No one is immune. It is part of our humanity. But we only have to be hurt once. Reliving the experience with a friend five minutes later, at the dinner table that evening, lying in bed that night, means that we are hurting ourselves three, four, five, or more times over. And as we indulge in brooding, we are actually placing the control of our lives into the hands of another person. And someone we don't like, at that! We are allowing that person to inhibit our sleep, our ability to enjoy food, our very health and happiness.

One of the beautiful traits of a child is relative freedom from grudges. Usually, fifteen minutes later, all is forgotten. In contrast, think of some miserable adults you know. Chances are, they are stewing over something that happened fifteen years ago! But let's get a little closer to home. As you read this paragraph, maybe you are unhappy because you have not forgotten something unpleasant that happened two weeks ago. Or even within the past twelve hours!

After the death of their father, Jacob, Joseph's brothers feared for their lives. But Joseph wept at even the thought of taking vengeance. His reply to their offer to be his slaves is a beautiful formula for understanding and rising above resentment: "Do not be afraid; is it for me to put myself in God's place? The evil you planned to do me has by God's design been turned to good, that he might bring about, as indeed he has, the deliverance of a numerous people" (Genesis 50:19–20 JB). To resent what has happened to you (circumstances) is to put yourself in God's place. Let God hold the reins. His design is to turn the evil to good.

Paul's great chapter on love contrasts love with resentment: "Nor does it [love] take account of a wrong that is suffered" (I Corinthians 13:5 NBV). The reverse of this is a good definition of resentment—taking account of a wrong that is suffered. Paul said in a letter to the Ephesian Christians, "When you are angry, commit no sin; do not remain angry until sundown" (Ephesians 4:26 NBV). Anger becomes resentment when it remains beyond sundown.

The psalmists often prayed for severe judgment upon their enemies. Perhaps this was a wrong attitude, but maybe not. Their example may have merit. Keep in mind that they are saying all this to *God*. Instead of repressing your resentment, or burdening your neighbor with it, integrate it into your prayer life. Some of these violent psalms take on new meaning when seen in this perspective.

One of your biggest allies in the resentment hassle is your sense of humor. Grow up! Learn to overlook, to assume that nothing was meant. And even if you're sure there was malice, cultivate the ability to be bigger, to see beyond a flimsy facade; into the heartache of the insecure, frightened person who wronged you. "It is . . . glory to overlook an offense," reads Proverbs 19:11 (NBV).

This is exactly what God does. He allows his sun to shine upon the just and the unjust.

Very much like a child, God does not bear grudges. "His anger lasts a moment; his favor lasts for life!" (Psalm 30:5 LB). You see, God's infinitude sees man as he is, in his temporary and pitiful existence. John Greenleaf Whittier discovered this truth. I would like to share with you his poem "Forgiveness":

My heart was heavy, for its trust had been
   Abused, its kindness answered with foul wrong;
So, turning gloomily from my fellowmen,
   One summer Sabbath day I strolled among
The green mounds of the village burial-place;
   Where, pondering how all human love and hate
   Find one sad level; and how, soon or late,
Wronged and wrongdoer, each with meekened face,
   And cold hands folded over a still heart,
Pass the green threshold of our common grave,
   Whither all footsteps tend, whence none depart,
Awed for myself, and pitying my race,
   Our common sorrow, like a mighty wave,
   Swept all my pride away, and trembling,
     I forgave!

4
GRAPPLERS, GRIPERS, AND GROUCHES

Neither do I believe God solves all our problems. In fact, I believe he gives us bigger and better ones! When people come to know God, life will not get easier, but it will get better.
—from *Life Is Tremendous*
by Charles "Tremendous" Jones

Grapplers, gripers, and grouches. Everyone you will meet today is one of the three. Out-and-out grouches are hard to find and probably aren't reading this book anyhow. Most people are gripers. They spend so much of their time fretting over things that nothing can be done about—the weather, taxes. Sharing a common gripe seems to be the "in" way to start a casual conversation these days. Grapplers are in another world. They will be found tackling controllable problems, things they can do something about.

In the Chinese language, the word *crisis* is represented by two interesting characters. The first character signifies "danger." But the second one denotes "opportunity."

A crisis is a danger point, true. But it can be an opportunity as well. It all depends on who is looking at it. Twisted paper used to cork bottles in a jail cell became the material on which Bunyan wrote *Pilgrim's Progress*. That's what I'm talking about.

In the place God had prepared for the Israelites, there were Amorites, Hittites, Perizzites, Canaanites, Hivites, and Jebusites. Entering the Promised Land always involves direct conflict with an enemy—or you might say, a crisis or problem. So often, we pray about a situation, and then expect God to lead us around the crisis; when he usually ends up leading us *through* "the valley of the shadow of death" (Psalm 23:4 KJV).

James says in his epistle, "Don't try to squirm out of your problems" (James 1:4 LB). Accept a problem as something to be solved, not bellyached about. Anyone can gripe. But it takes effort to fight and work. And when it's all over, the escape artist usually expends more energy than the one who faces the music, anyhow.

It's debatable whether we grow at all unless we are grappling with a problem. Moreover, the habit of running from unpleasant confrontations may only be another road which leads eventually to emotional illness.

The psalmist prayed, "When my heart is overwhelmed, lead me to the rock that is higher than I" (Psalm 61:2 NBV).

Read that again.

When we are overwhelmed, this is the time for growth.

It was in the night when Yahweh called Gideon, and we later find him going up the Nomad's Way to capture the kings of Midian. God didn't prevent the snake from biting Paul. But it didn't poison him. The Israelites had walls of water on either side and the Egyptians in pursuit, a hair-raising experience!

Don't expect immunity from emergencies, tight situations, and problems. But do expect deliverance.

There's a difference.

5
WORRY IN REVERSE

Men become courageous by the same process that they become fearful; successful and confident by the same process that they become failures. Both are ideas that we sell ourselves. If you are timid and fearful or feel inferior, you do not need to learn the technique of selling ideas to yourself. You are already a past master at the art. All you need do is change the ideas you sell. Suggest confidence to yourself in exactly the same way you have been suggesting failure.
—from *The Wealth Within You* by Elmer Wheeler

The mother of Tobias went out every day to look down the road for her lost son. Her husband, Tobit, tried to comfort her, but to no avail. We read that she would weep and moan all night, unable to sleep. But the actual facts were: her son was not only safe, but he had found a wife, and God was about to heal her husband's blindness. The words of the text in the book of Tobit (10:7 JB) comprise a good definition of worry: "She trusted no eyes but her own."

We're all too familiar with the worry-failure-worry-failure merry-go-round. Worry causes more failure. And more failure adds to the worries. It's got to help us, to just stop for a minute and analyze what we are actually doing when we worry. I'll tell you what you are doing. You are using your imagination to visualize unfortunate events in the future, most of which will never happen.

I have a suggestion. Why not use the same mental process and begin to visualize all the wonderful things that are going to happen? The Bible calls this "vision"—worry in reverse. And it makes me no great prophet when I say that good days are ahead. God will be alive and working tomorrow, and the next day, and the next.

Gems like these from Psalm 104 can help sharpen this vision: "He placed streams that gush from the mountains. . . . He . . . fills the earth with fruit. . . . There are . . . vegetables and grain for man to cultivate, wine to make him glad, and olive oil as lotion for his skin, and bread to give him strength. . . . O Lord . . . the earth is full of your riches" (Psalm 104:10–24 LB). Open your eyes and bury your worries!

To worry means to assume a responsibility God never intended us to have. You see, we aren't qualified. Alvin Toffler in *Future Shock* warns that, in thinking about the future, we are worrying about precisely the wrong things. And this is what makes worry so futile. We don't know enough about the future to know what to worry about!

Practicing vision delivers what you might call side benefits as well. Most humans want to improve—to be better persons. We all know people trying to lose weight, quit smoking, etc. Did you know that there are two basic ways to reach for goals of self-improvement? One almost always works and the other almost never does. You can grit your teeth and exert sheer willpower—a method quite contrary to basic human nature. But after that has failed, don't despair. There's another way. And that is to catch a vision of some*thing* or some*one* greater than yourself. This is exactly how Jesus affects our lives. We catch a vision of his beauty and holiness. The apostle Paul observed in II Corinthians 3:18 that if we behold the glory of the Lord, we are changed into his likeness.

Imagination is a blessing sent from God. Worry turns this blessing into a curse. But with God-given vision, it can become our friend once again.

Vision.

Worry in reverse.

6

SERENDIPITY!

Rising or setting, the sun looks the same. So it is in life—these experiences come upon us that change our lives. . . . It is so easy to feel that everything is lost, that life from now on will not be worth living. But it may be—it often is—that which we thought was the setting of the sun may be the sunrise. . . . What seemed to be the end may be a new beginning.
      —from *All Things Are Possible Through Prayer*
         by Charles Allen

Once there lived a young man who ordered a book on photography. The publisher made a mistake and sent a book on ventriloquism instead. This was a disappointment, as it would be to any boy. But the youngster decided to study the book anyhow. And thus began Edgar Bergen's exciting career.

Sam Clemens went west to look for gold. He ran short of money, so he found a job as a reporter on the Virginia City, Nevada, newspaper. While working there, the idea came to him for the "Jumping Frog" story. And soon the whole country was asking, "Who is this Mark Twain?"

The apostle Paul planned a journey to Spain but ended up in a Roman prison. A carefully planned evangelistic tour had gone down the drain, so Paul did the next best thing. He wrote a few letters to his fellow believers in different parts of the world.

Serendipity, a word coined by Horace Walpole, is defined as "accidentally finding unexpected things while working on something else." Disappointment can mean serendipity. My three little stories bear witness to that. Maybe you will become number four! For it could be happening to you right now, though it may be some time before you see it clearly.

Realistically, happiness has to be serendipity or it doesn't happen at all. The surest way not to be happy is to drop everything and go looking for it! It has to look for you. You can't look for it. Observe the truly happy man. You'll probably find him busy doing what has to be done. He might be simply taking time with the children right now. And even though he doesn't get paid, and even though the doing may be a little inconvenient, this man is living in a world of happiness unknown to those who make a career out of pleasure-seeking.

In *Man's Search for Meaning*, psychotherapist Viktor Frankl goes so far as to say, "A forced intention makes impossible what one forcibly wishes. . . . The more a man tries to demonstrate his sexual potency or a woman her ability to experience orgasm, the less they are able to succeed. Pleasure is, and must remain, a side effect or by-product, and is destroyed and spoiled to the degree to which it is made a goal in itself."

We say, "If only I had an Aladdin's lamp" (and some think prayer is one of these!). But that's part of the problem. We just don't know what is best for us or what we really want. The old saying is closer to the truth than we realize—"If a man could have half his wishes, he would double his troubles."

The other day I stumbled across serendipity in the writings of Paul: "Be not forgetful to entertain strangers, for thereby some have entertained angels unawares" (Hebrews 13:2 KJV). And most people do try to make life too predictable. Let's face it. *We just don't know when our greatest moments will come.* Isaiah speaks of God working "unexpected miracles" (Isaiah 64:3 JB). God is full of surprises, and we might say that life with him is

serendipity forever! But not always in a way that we expect, or that is immediately pleasurable.

These lines, which I found in *The Christian Reader*
magazine, should challenge you. They did me.

We ask for strength, and God gives us difficulties
which make us strong.
We pray for wisdom, and God sends us problems,
the solution of which develops wisdom.
We plead for prosperity—
and God gives us brain and brawn to work.
We plead for courage,
and God gives us dangers to overcome.
We ask for favors—
God gives us opportunities.

7
TOUCHSTONE FEVER

*My best lessons in life are not those teaching me
new things so much as those helping me unlearn
some old things.*
—from *Life Is Tremendous*
by Charles "Tremendous" Jones

Ever hear the story of the Touchstone? Briefly, here it is.

When the great library of Alexandria burned, one book
was saved. But it was not a valuable book. So a poor man,
who could read a little, bought it for a few coppers. It
was not very interesting, but lying between the pages was
a thin strip of parchment which contained the secret of
the Touchstone (a magic stone which turned all that it
touched to gold. Except the owner, of course). The poor
man sold his few belongings, bought some simple supplies,
and journeyed to a certain beach on the Black Sea. He
would know the Touchstone immediately, because it would
feel warm in his hand. So he began testing pebbles, throwing them down when they felt cold. But he soon realized
that this method wouldn't do, for he might pick up the
same stone hundreds of times. And that was when he
devised the plan to throw all cold pebbles, not down at
his feet, but into the sea. A week went by, a month, a
year, three years. One morning he was walking along as
usual, picked up a pebble . . . cold . . . threw it in the sea,
picked up a pebble . . . cold . . . threw it in the sea, picked
up a pebble . . . warm . . . *threw it into the sea!* He had
formed the habit of throwing them into the sea, and when

the one he wanted came along, he threw that one away, too.

Here we have, represented, a universal human problem. We have tried so many things; have tossed away so many cold stones. Then along comes Jesus, the Touchstone, with his warm offer of everlasting life, and now, being slaves to years of disappointment, we toss him into the sea as well. So, the need to *repent*, to change.

Thomas Edison claimed that we don't know one-tenth of 1 percent about anything. This is especially true in the area of understanding the Bible and living a life of joy and peace. Alvin Toffler urges students to learn how to discard old ideas. Tomorrow's illiterate will not be the man who can't read; he will be the man who has not learned how to learn.

In the wicked man of Psalm 36 is portrayed the opposite of repentance. "He sees himself with too flattering an eye to detect and detest his guilt . . . he has turned his back on wisdom. . . . He never rejects what is bad" (Psalm 36:2-4 JB). The man who "sees himself with too flattering an eye" is standing still, and has turned away from God. Toffler's illiterate of the future.

So many people's lives are only a parade of immediate rewards and immediate chastisements. These people have merely learned how to get immediate results and avoid immediate pain. Then they proceed to label this talent "experience," or even "wisdom." But what they really have cultivated is a false instinct for safety and surface security!

The fact is, we must change. And so often that is the last thing we want to do! The Bible describes this moment in Peter's life so tenderly: "As he [Peter] considered that, he wept audibly" (Mark 14:72 NBV). A man weeping audibly is a rare sight. But when a man really considers how far he has missed the mark, weeping will not be difficult.

In *Daily Celebration*, William Barclay tells a story about

a mother whose son had been killed in war. She was visited by an angel who offered to let her see her son for five minutes. But she must choose the moment in his life that she wished to see. After much thought, the mother said slowly, "I would have him for five minutes as he was one day when he ran in from the garden to ask my forgiveness for being naughty. He was so small and so unhappy, and the tears were making streaks down his face through the garden dust. And he flew to my arms with such force that he hurt me."

It just may be that this is the moment in our lives that God cherishes the most. When we *repent*—and run to his loving, waiting arms.

8
WHAT IS IT?

*I think our present outlook might be like that of a
small boy who, on being told that the sexual act was
the highest bodily pleasure, should immediately ask
whether you ate chocolates at the same time. On receiving the answer "No" he might regard absence of
chocolates as the chief characteristic of sexuality. In
vain would you tell him that the reason why lovers
in their carnal raptures don't bother about chocolates
is that they have something better to think of. The
boy knows chocolates; he does not know the positive
thing that excludes it.*

—from *Miracles* by C. S. Lewis

Man's greatest failure. His inability to appreciate what
God wants to do for him. In the wilderness, the Israelites'
first reaction to the food Yahweh provided for them was
to exclaim, "What is it?" Consequently, "it" acquired the
name "manna," which literally means "What is it?" Even
today, this is a typical reaction to what God is offering to
man.

Louis Armstrong once said about jazz, "If I have to
explain it to you, then you ain't got it." It's that way with
love. Walking up to a young couple and trying to "explain" love is a good way to feel foolish real quick!

I'll be honest with you. I can't "prove" that there is a
God. I can't even prove that I know God. But, for that
matter, neither can you prove that a sunset is beautiful,
that your mother loves you, even that you feel good today.

We all experience many, many realities every day that it would be foolish to try to prove.

Jesus referred to this new level of awareness in the spirit world and compared it to being "born again." We need to see that "reason" and "proof" are not always the final word.

The apocryphal book of Wisdom provides further insight into the nature of manna, by saying it contained every delight, and satisfied every taste, "for, conforming to the taste of whoever ate it, it transformed itself into what each eater wished" (Wisdom 16:21 JB). Amazing. You know, the experience of knowing God is like that. Jesus miraculously becomes just what we need and desire in our innermost selves,

John the Baptist referred to Jesus as "One who stands among you, whom you do not recognize" (John 1:27 NBV). That was almost two thousand years ago. And the world hasn't changed much.

Like the small boy, all we can see is the chocolates. And God comes along, and we open our mouths and say something stupid like, "What is it?"

9
HOPE

As long as one has God, there is always something else to do. No matter how bad yesterday may have been or today is, with God there is a good tomorrow ahead.
—from *All Things Are Possible Through Prayer*
  by Charles Allen

Let's not kid ourselves. This failure business can get plenty rough at times. That is why hope is so important— one of the "three things that remain" when all else has vanished. In times of distress, hope can be the only thing that pulls us through.

Of all books, the Bible is a book chock full of hope. Verse after verse, story upon story, the message is there. Written on the pages. Written between the lines. Sinner or saint, there is always hope. There is hope, if we'll look to Jesus.

Here are a few examples: "If you have hope, this will make you cheerful" (Romans 12:12 JB). "It is good . . . to hope . . . for the salvation of the Lord" (Lamentations 3:26 LB). And finally Paul again: "May the God of hope bring you such joy and peace in your faith that the power of the Holy Spirit will remove all bounds to hope" (Romans 15:13 JB).

Paul and Jeremiah. Of all Bible characters, these two men lived in circumstances the least conducive to hope. But hope is like that. It's at its best when there is no human reason for it. As the Israelites were going into exile, God instructed them to mark well the way, to set up guideposts, because they would be coming back the same way (Jeremiah 31:31).

Viktor Frankl, writing of his experiences in a Nazi prison camp, recalls, "I had no intention of losing hope and giving up. For no man knew what the future would bring, much less the next hour!" Why shouldn't this outlook and attitude prevail in our everyday problems and struggles? We all have something to wake up to every morning of our lives—another chance. It is always time to hope. It is always time to anticipate.

Proverbs, the Christian's personal handbook on daily living, gives us an inspiring picture of hope taken from nature: "The lizards, they are easy to catch and kill, yet are found even in king's palaces!" (Proverbs 30:28 LB). If a lizard can make the palace, there's hope for you and me!

Be certain, however, that your hope is broad enough. We get involved in small details and are disappointed when life doesn't "jibe" with our preconceived plan. The idea is to center our hope on the ultimate goal, whatever that may be, not on the road we might prefer to travel to get there.

One of Robert Louis Stevenson's poems, "The Lamplighter," comes from the experiences of his childhood. On winter evenings, this sickly child loved to watch the lamplighter on his rounds, climbing the ladder, leaving a glow of light behind. And so Stevenson wrote:

> But I, when I am stronger
>   and can choose what I'm to do,
> O Leerie, I'll go round at night
>   and light the lamps with you!

Build your hope.
Never, never, never destroy your hope.

THIRTY MINUTES OR THIRTY YEARS

While browsing through a store I came across a book with the title, "Shortcut to Success." Son, there ain't no shortcut to success! . . . Such suggestions don't make their appeal to a man's strength but to his weakness. This is one of the things wrong with people. They want the kind of success that comes without cost. So they spend all their days looking for shortcuts and easy ways. . . . Real success is working, creating. It's dreaming and making dreams come true. You can't have that kind of success without sweating over it. You can't continue to make opportunities and develop ideas without paying a price. The price is hard thinking, planning and working.
—from Richard Brannon's Notebook

"Every man is enthusiastic at times," writes Edward B. Butler in an issue of *Catholic Layman* magazine. "One man has enthusiasm for thirty minutes, another for thirty days, but it is the man who has it for thirty years who makes a success of his life!"

Almost all gospel preaching today is geared to decision-making. "Have you made your decision for Christ?" is a question oft repeated. And decisions are important. We need to decide to serve Jesus.

But maybe there's something more crucial than deciding. One of Jesus' parables I call the parable for the twentieth century. In this parable the Master compares the servant who "decides" and then doesn't go, with the one who, after saying no, eventually does his master's

will. How could it be put more clearly? Obedience, walking daily with God, this is "where it's at." "He that shall
endure unto the end, the same shall be saved."

In *Daily Celebration* William Barclay recounts this true
story. A group of people were talking about heroism. "A
young man turned to an old woman; she looked so ordinary and so serene; he did not know that life had been for
her a series of tragic things. 'And what kind of heroism
do you practice?' he said with an obvious air of thinking
that he did not believe that there could be any kind of
heroism in a life like hers. "I?' she said. 'I practice the
heroism of *going on.'*"

George Bernard Shaw's plan called for writing five pages
each day. And he went right on with that plan for nine
frustrating years. He made a total of thirty dollars in
that time—about a penny a day!

Jesus set down a beautiful formula for developing this
rare quality of perseverance. Ask. Seek. Knock. We might
break it down this way. Ask (pray about it), seek (study
the Bible for guidance), knock (act). The man who asks
and knocks without seeking (Bible) is in danger of taking
off in the wrong direction, of becoming a fanatic. The
man who seeks and knocks without asking, without a disciplined prayer life, becomes the cold "organization man."
And finally, when we ask and seek without knocking
(action), we are just plain lazy!

Pure laziness is so often the real culprit. And the con-
foundedness of it all lies in the fact that laziness is the
last vice any man will own up to!

Ask, seek, knock. It takes all three. And we must keep
at it day after day after day.

Observe a child learning to walk. He falls down, gets
up, falls down, gets up. Have you ever seen one give up
and quit? He naturally gets up, probably because no one
has told him there is a choice! Approach life this way
every day, with the same concentration and patience. It
won't be long before you will notice the difference.

THE MAN I MIGHT HAVE BEEN

*A man . . . suddenly sees the vast sweep of God's
design in life, and observes the cheap and discordant
little effort his own living so far represents when
seen against that background. That is real conviction
of sin.*
—from *Your God Is Too Small* by J. B. Phillips

Failure is good if it opens the mind to the possibility of
something better. We catch a glimpse of the "man I might
have been." We wake up one morning to realize that we
have been settling for less than the best. And that can be
the widest gap in the world—the difference between what
I am and what I could be.

Sometimes this gap can have tragic results. The city
next to ours in Maryland is called Rockville. Back in the
thirties, a train–school bus accident there took the lives
of fifteen schoolchildren. There was no signal at the
crossing, but there was a watchman, who was due to stay
till midnight, but got sleepy and went home early. Someone remarked that they wondered if he'd ever sleep again.

And we need to recognize our shortcomings without
thinking of ourselves as worthless because of them. When
an expensive violin gets out of tune, we don't toss it into
the nearest wastebasket. We simply tune it. Violins can
be tuned. So can human beings.

Jesus demonstrated this attitude toward human shortcomings. We are all familiar with his scathing words to
Peter—"Get thee behind me, Satan" (Matthew 16:23

KJV). But did you know that just *six days later*, Peter was one of the three chosen to witness the Transfiguration? God does not hold things against us. He forgives. And forgets.

A frequent sight in the African bush is a lion feeding on an antelope. What that lion doesn't know is that if antelopes would team up, they could trample him to death in a matter of seconds. But there's one catch. The antelope doesn't know it either! So, the years will roll on and lions will continue to devour antelopes. I don't expect that to change.

But you and I are more than lions and antelopes. We see situations and circumstances in our lives that we know can be better. The question with man is not "Can he change?" but "How badly does he want to change?"

Football coach George Allen sums up his philosophy thus: "Any group of athletes who are willing to accept less than the best will end up with less than the best." Life is not a harmless diversion or a chance adventure. It is the "big one," the crucial game that we play just once. And after you make the play-offs, there are no ties. The big games all must of necessity end in victory or defeat.

Win the biggest game of all. Start today to become the "man I might have been."

OUR FEELINGS

12
FEELING LIKE IT

Big men became big by doing what they didn't want to do when they didn't want to do it.
—from *Have a Good Day* magazine

For so many on the earth today, life has become a spectator sport. If we know what's happening, if we are aware, then we are satisfied. But being aware, being informed, is not enough. The question is, are we just watching things happen around us or are we making things happen? Unfortunately, most of us are watching the world go by. And it doesn't have to be that way.

Primarily, we're getting hung up on our *feelings*. Let me give you a simple test. Do you wait until you *feel* compassionate before helping someone? Do you wait until you *feel* spiritual to pray or read the Bible? If so, then I've got news for you. You are part of that great throng of individuals who watch things happen.

To think that we have to feel a certain thing before we do it is a fatal mistake. You see, this is exactly backwards. The idea is to decide what has to be done in a given situation, and do it—then you will probably feel like it after you do it, not before.

I'll illustrate. Suppose you are alone in a room in your home, and some music that irritates you is playing on the stereo. What do you do? Do you pull your hair out? Curse your fate? Give up on the day? Of course not. You simply walk over to the set and either change the record or turn it off. You possess (potentially) the same power over your moods. It is all a matter of choice. And the choice belongs to you.

We hear people say, "He made me get angry!" or "So-and-so ruined my day." Not so. Nobody can make you feel anything. You choose to get angry, have your feelings hurt, get disgusted—or, to be patient, understanding.

This idea occurs again and again in the Bible. From Proverbs: "Gentle words cause life and health; griping brings discouragement" (Proverbs 15:4 LB). "When a man is gloomy, everything seems to go wrong; when he is cheerful, everything seems right!" (Proverbs 15:15 LB).

The goal is not to eliminate moods, but to control them. To have moods is simply to have personality. But to be moody is just plain old egotism.

Be realistic. People do not excel at things only when they are in the mood. Once you decide where you are going in life, then you go. Another word for this is *discipline.*

You go. Feelings or no feelings.

13
WHO WILL ROLL AWAY THE STONE?

You gain faith, not by argument, but by action. . . .
A lot of people try to be too intellectual in their re-
ligion. . . . Jesus did not give us the reasons why
faith moves mountains; He simply said, "Have faith
in God."
        —from *All Things Are Possible Through Prayer*
        by Charles Allen

On Easter Sunday morning, the three women (Mary Magdalene, the other Mary, and Salome) said to each other, as they contemplated their visit to the tomb, "Who will roll away the stone for us from the entrance to the tomb?" (Mark 16:3 JB). But (and here's the secret) they still went!

I don't know why, but I know it's true that God doesn't just move in, take over our problems and make things right. The answers come as we *act*. This is consistent with our emotional makeup. W. Clement Stone explains in *Success Unlimited* magazine: "Emotions (like fear) are not immediately subject to reason, but they are subject to action. When thoughts do not neutralize an undesirable emotion, action will." For instance, you'll never reason your way out of lust, but there are things you can do.

A misconception prevails among Christians today which associates aggressiveness with lack of dependence on God. Jehovah assured Joshua before he left to rescue Gibeon that he would be victorious. But he still had to march all night long to bring about the victory. And this same Joshua passed on to the descendants of Joseph, the tribes of Ephraim and Manasseh, these words: "A mountain shall be yours; it is covered with woods. but you must clear it" (Joshua 17:18 JB). Barclay in *Daily Celebration* refers to "a kind of delusion that things can happen without work."

St. John recorded these words of Christ: "If ye know these things, happy are ye if ye do them" (John 13:17 KJV). This is where Jesus finds most of us today. Our problem is not ignorance. We know about Jesus. We know what the Bible says. We're just not doing.

The Christian life is a *walk*, not mostly talk. Let's place the accent where Jesus himself put it—on the walking. Today's overemphasis on "profession of faith" can be misleading. The danger is that we make a hero out of the man who wears his religion on his lapel. But God alone sees into the heart of a man.

Paul believed that the kingdom of God is not "just talking; it is living by God's power" (I Corinthians 4:20 LB). When Jesus calls, he first demands our obedient action: "Leave the nets . . . sell what you have . . . abandon the house of custom . . . follow thou me." We must have faith. Let there be no doubt about that. But faith apart from works only appears in books, never in real life.

Possibly, even as you read these lines, you can sense this same Jesus speaking to you. He is alive in the world today, you know. Respond to his call by *doing*. Your response can revolutionize your life!

The lepers outside the city of Samaria were astonished to find that God was working as they got up and did something about their plight (II Kings 7:3). And this just might be the very thing that will unleash God's power in your life—to begin to do what you feel God wants you to do.

A good decision, without action, becomes merely a good intention. A vague desire to be a better person is not enough. You've got to pin it down.

And once you do, you'll discover something.

14
WHAT IS THAT IN THINE HAND?

When General William Booth, the founder of the
Salvation Army, went blind, his son Bramwell broke
the news to him that he would never see again. . . .
The old man's hand moved across the counterpane
until it grasped his son's. "Bramwell," he said, "I
have done what I could for God and for the people
with my eyes. Now I shall do what I can for God and
for the people without my eyes."
                                    —Harry Emerson Fosdick

Deep truths and insights often come to us in the form of a
question. Recall how often Jesus replied to a question
with another question. God broke his silence to Job with
a barrage of piercing questions. That ought to teach us a
lesson about life. Most of the time, it is more important
to ask the right questions than to dole out a series of
answers. Answers can be so shallow. We should strive
rather for understanding.

Jehovah's words to Moses, "What is that in thine
hand?" (Exodus 4:2 KJV) are a good question with which
to start a new day. Opportunity can alight nearby in the
midst of seemingly ordinary circumstances. We all need
to develop a sensitivity to the presence of opportunity.
When good fortune comes, you aren't likely to hear a
trumpet blast or be rapped on the head. It will probably
only whisper. And maybe only once.

A handicapped man was asked the question "Doesn't
being lame color your life?" He made a wonderful reply:
"Yes, but thank God I can choose the color!" Jesus con-

cludes his great Sermon on the Mount with the story of the two houses built on sand and rock. Note that the same rain, floods, and wind beat on both. It's not circumstances, but how we build, that counts.

Something happens to a person when he quits whining, when he stops blaming other people, when he starts to use circumstances as a means of growth. The "me-and-my-problems" Christian is a paradox. Are you a Christian? Do you realize that as a Christian you have already chosen daily identification with the cross to which Jesus was nailed? The heartache and the suffering of the world, not just his own, is the Christian's responsibility. And there's plenty of it. Just look around you.

"What is that in thine hand?" God has placed in our hands a power. He has handed us the controls. "Whatsoever ye shall loose on earth shall be loosed in heaven" (Matthew 18:18 KJV). Today's Jesus People disturb me a little in this respect. Everything that happens to and around a Christian can't just be conveniently labeled "God's will." Even the oft-quoted Romans 8:28 implies that after something happens, we still must choose to let God work it together for good.

We've all been too fatalistic. We need to go back and read the stories of the Bible through different eyes. More often than not, opportunities were captured by those who dared to attack—David and Goliath, Elijah on Mount Carmel.

You can throw a Joseph in jail, but before long he will be in charge of all the prisoners. And years later, Joseph named his second son Ephraim ("doubly fruitful"), "because," he said, "God has made me fruitful in the country of my misfortune" (Genesis 41:52 JB).

Some of us are like the sick man at the pool of Bethesda. And Jesus jolts us with the question "Do you want to get well?" (John 5:6 NBV). Situations such as sickness and failure can be too comfortable.

Caleb returned from spying out the Promised Land with

words of reassurance for the people: "Let us go up at once and possess it, for we are well able to conquer it!" (Numbers 13:30 LB). But Caleb's advice was spurned, and so, they had the forty years of wanderings. As Grover Cleveland observed, "Seeing opportunity and seizing it are two different relations." How true.

As long as we continue to wait for the time to be right to start doing something worthwhile, we will lead mediocre lives. The time will never be just right. Start where you stand! Work with what tools you have!

These lines are from "Invictus" by William Ernest Henley, who was ill most of his life:

> It matters not how strait the gate
> How charged with punishments the scroll,
> I am the master of my fate;
> I am the captain of my soul.

"What is that in thine hand?"

15
BRIDGE OVER TROUBLED WATER

*I consider it a dangerous misconception of mental
hygiene to assume that what man needs in the first
place is equilibrium or, as it is called in biology,
"homeostasis," i.e., a tensionless state. What man
actually needs is not a tensionless state but rather
the striving and struggling for some goal worthy of
him. What he needs is not the discharge of tension
at any cost, but the call of a potential meaning waiting to be fulfilled by him.*

—from *Man's Search for Meaning*
by Viktor E. Frankl

When we are controlled by our feelings, when we go up
and down with the tide of what people say or don't say,
or other circumstances, we are, whether we realize it or
not, faithfully practicing for our role as escape artists.
Escape has become a full-time occupation for so many.

Paul Simon, of Simon and Garfunkel, says himself that
he was not writing seriously, but just composing a pretty
tune, when he wrote "Bridge over Troubled Water"—and
I'll take his word for it. Still, I feel that his song comes
across to the public as highly symbolic. Each of us decides
what will be our "bridge over troubled water." Drugs,
alcohol, sex for the sake of sex—the lyrics fit each one,
or rather, what each one promises.

Someone has said, and everyone has noticed, that the
slaves of the senses, after the first bait, are starved by
their masters. We see this happening to a drug addict and

we say, "How sad." But the truth is, there are countless other seemingly innocent escape routes which also starve us. And, just as surely, we become their slaves. The only difference is that the process is slower and more subtle, and thus harder to detect.

When we adults compulsively turn to the TV set or the refrigerator to offset boredom, we are demonstrating to our children the need for an escape. When we turn instead to the Carpenter from Nazareth, we demonstrate to them our willingness to face reality, to tackle life on a challenging day-to-day basis. (And I see a world of difference between deciding to watch a specific TV program, and just letting the set run on and on, with no purpose but to watch TV. Ditto trips to the refrigerator.)

There is much talk and controversy over marijuana today. Even if there were no harmful side effects, I would still put it in the same bag as sexual self-gratification. Anything that is a habitual escape from reality has to be harmful, if only for that reason. There is always the danger that later on we will find ourselves unable to cope with the real world.

We are human and we all need diversion. I don't mean to imply that we don't. But diversion does not have to be perversion. Diversions such as sports, comics and comedy, and hobbies, are by and large creative. Recreation. In the very definition of the word is found the difference.

The angel at the tomb said, "Why seek ye the living among the dead?" (Luke 24:5 KJV). How often we each find ourselves doing just that. With the things we do. And don't do.

Critics who label Jesus just another escape route are of the armchair variety. Because, when we turn to Jesus as our "bridge over troubled water," we find that we are no longer running away. We find ourselves face-to-face with reality.

Reality with a capital R.

16
THE ONE-EYED MAN

*You must learn to live each moment fully; you must
learn to heighten your feeling about the little things
that make life exciting. There can be joy in biting
into your scrambled eggs . . . you must rediscover life
feelings like these.*
  —Maxwell Maltz in *Success Unlimited* magazine

Amaziah was king of Judah for twenty-nine years. We
read about him: "He did what is pleasing to Yahweh,
though not wholeheartedly" (II Chronicles 25:2 JB). There
is a universal need today for the one-eyed man—the man
who will concentrate on one purpose in life. That's what
Jesus alluded to when he said, "If therefore thine eye be
single, thy whole body shall be full of light" (Matthew
6:22 KJV).

Did you ever meet someone who's always doing the
next thing? Once I left out two songs and cut a concert
ten minutes short because of a restless pastor in the front
pew who had confided that he was leaving immediately
after the program to drive all night to another state.

Live fully in the present! Don't be always thinking of
the next thing to be done. Do what you are doing right
now. It sounds super-simple until you try it!

Children are masters of the art of concentration. But
concentration is rare in the adult world. We do so many
things at once—listen to the radio, talk, smoke, eat, drink.

To concentrate on others means primarily to be able to
listen. It's so easy to "listen" to someone, and even answer

52

appropriately, without really listening. Along with listening comes the ability to be interested. Be known as an interested person. Don't be afraid to even become excited once in a while!

The lustful, roving eye implies a lack of concentration. God so constructed man emotionally that sexual satisfaction will forever elude the man or woman who does not concentrate his or her desires on one person, and only one. Playboys get into their thirties and wake up one day to discover that they can't really fall in love with anyone anymore. They have sacrificed forever the deep joys of a one man–one woman lifetime love affair, for the sake of variety, the so-called spice of life. But you can't have concentration and variety at the same time. It's always one or the other.

Above all else, we need to concentrate when we pray. Prayer specialist Frank Laubach quips, "If your prayers are boring you, quite likely they are boring God, too." Three-by-five-inch index cards have helped make my prayer time more efficient. After all, it's the intensity of our prayers that gets results, not the amount of time we put in.

And we desperately need to pray. The Fifth Psalm tells us that when we fail to pray, we actually break an appointment with God! That's how important it is to him.

In *The Art of Loving* Erich Fromm divides the learning of any art into three stages: first, mastery of theory; second, mastery of practice; and third and most important, "the mastery of the art must be a matter of ultimate concern; there must be nothing else in the world more important than the art." Concentration again. How important is it to you? How intense is your desire?

Jesus taught that if your right eye offends you, pluck it out and cast it from you. Personally, I learned my greatest lesson here quite literally. An auto accident took away the sight in my right eye. And this boy did some very serious thinking about how I had been using two eyes, and about what changes were necessary in order to rededicate the one eye I had left.

Be a one-eyed man. Learn to concentrate. And in both ways. Concentrate on the activity of the moment. Develop a concentrated life purpose.

Go one step beyond the Judean king. Not only do what is pleasing to God, but do it wholeheartedly.

17
THE RESEARCH DEPARTMENT

Every salesman would be wise to set aside 30 minutes each day for research and meditation on the real meaning of his capabilities, with a definite purpose to improve his ability and to uncover the spiritual power that will help him. . . . The prophet wisely counsels in Lamentations (3:40), "Let us search and try our ways, and turn again to the Lord." Because of the pressure and pace of activity, you may be tempted to think that you lack the time or opportunity. . . . The research department has certainly benefited the large industrial concerns—and the time you spend in exploring the undiscovered regions inside your mind is going to be worth a lot of cash, and also a lot of true enjoyment.
—from *The Power of Creative Selling*
by Earl Prevette

When General Dwight Eisenhower flew to England to take supreme command of the British and American forces he had only one book on the plane with him—the Holy Bible.

Why do we need the Bible? Solomon wrote his proverbs "to teach his people how to live—how to act in every circumstance" (Proverbs 1:2 LB). What will the Bible do for me? "Then wisdom will be given you, and knowledge of God himself" (Proverbs 2:5 LB). And what good is wisdom? "A wise man is mightier than a strong man. Wisdom is mightier than strength" (Proverbs 24:5 LB).

The man who studies the Bible regularly isn't the one who loses interest. It's the casual reader who gets bored. Of course, the way some of the more archaic translations are laid out looks almost like a conspiracy against reading it! I challenge you, though, to find a suitable translation and begin to dig. You'll strike gold. That's a guarantee. But you have to stay with it. The psalmist spoke of "meditating all day on your Law" and then said, "Now I have come to love it" (Psalm 119:97 JB).

However, the Bible will be something less than what it can be to you, if you allow yourself to become (1) overwhelmed by the book itself, (2) overfamiliar with the message, or (3) overconcerned with small detail. Let's attack these one at a time.

It was Albert Einstein who concluded, "The most incomprehensible thing about the universe is that it is comprehensible." We look up at the stars at night and we are overwhelmed. And rightly so. God's creation is mind-staggering. But Einstein reminds us that all this wonder is reducible to a few simple laws and a few simple equations. And, to him, this is the greatest miracle of all.

Likewise, when we pick up the Bible and read of the Creation, of Moses at the Red Sea, Peter and John at the temple gate, we can be tempted to despair. How could this apply to poor little me? But then is the time to employ a slight paraphrase of Einstein—the most incomprehensible thing about God, about the Bible, is that it is comprehensible! We can bring it down to one simple formula—that is, God cares about man. God loves the world. God even has a plan for your life! "My hand has made both earth and skies, and they are mine. Yet I will look with pity on the man who has a humble and a contrite heart, who trembles at my word." God said that to Isaiah (Isaiah 66:2 LB).

The Bible's familiarity can also block some of the great truths from our minds. Chesterton advises us to look at familiar objects till they seem strange, that is to say, till we actually see them, instead of being told how to see them. Apply this to your handling of the Bible.

For example, when I say, "For God so loved the world, that he gave his only begotten Son . . ." what is the first thing that pops into your mind? Almost inevitably, the answer comes back, "Why, John 3:16, of course." And that is the answer I got from audiences time after time until one night in Avon, New York, a twelve-year-old Catholic boy in the front row of a Protestant church blurted out, "That reminds me of the crucifixion." Beautiful. "For God so loved . . ." should say to us today, first and foremost, "This is Jesus speaking. He is speaking of himself. And we ought to listen."

Then there is the fact that a few centuries after Jesus spoke those words, some scholars came up with the chapter-verse idea (admittedly convenient!), which results in this significant saying of Jesus falling in the third chapter and the sixteenth verse of John's Gospel.

Be careful. Rattling off isolated Scripture verses can not only sound like a spelling bee, it can amount to a distortion. And it tends to depersonalize the message that is there.

Constant dissection and close scrutiny of the Bible can also derail the message. Emerson observed, "The world can never be learned by learning all its details." It is important to step back and look at the full picture. This is why certain commentaries distract me fiercely!

Let me illustrate. Emanuel Leutze's popular painting *Washington Crossing the Delaware* depicts the dramatic events of Christmas night, 1776. However, investigation will reveal that the Betsy Ross flag shown in the painting had not even been designed in 1776! This slipup counts for little, though, when you think of the inspiration this painting is to all Americans. We see here how inspiration is infinitely more important than technical perfection.

And so with the Bible. The many translations reveal that the human element is present as God attempts to get his message through. But this should not in any way diminish the fact that this book of books is God's Holy Word. Beware. You'll never comprehend the Bible by overattention to small details.

Reread the quotation at the beginning of this chapter. Can Christians get by with less?

18

THE FORGOTTEN WORD

I remembered when I was a small boy waking up early on Spring mornings and smelling the freshness of the earth and dreaming about those things life might have in store . . . even that day. Then, as I had grown up, I had "put away childish things" and had learned that life was hard and one did not live in continual expectancy. But, now as a grown man with a family, I began waking up and smelling the earth again. I kept waiting for this expectancy to go away, but it never has.
   —from *The Taste of New Wine* by Keith Miller

During a church league softball game last summer, a train went by. No one seemed to notice. We were all taken up with something more important (the "reel" world, as Marshall McLuhan calls it!). Except for one small boy on the sidelines, whose spontaneous outburst was the epitome of wonder! The boy's absorption (clapping his hands, running, shouting repeatedly) so arrested my attention that I still see it all so vividly. At the time, I found myself envying that child and his world, so full of awe and just plain life.

Some humans need to be reminded that God colored the world, a fact that should stare us all in the face. Emerson wrote, "I defy your straitlaced, weary social ways and modes. Blue is the sky, green the fields and groves, fresh the springs, glad the rivers, and hospitable the splendor of sun and star." We don't have to manufacture excitement and thrills. They're all around us. It's our eyes, not what we "see," that are the problem.

Whereas adults regard it as a sign of weakness to be surprised or awed, the child cultivates this experience. And if you look for it, you too can find excitement—even in the commonplace. But first you have to look.

To a young man on the flying trapeze, a veteran circus performer volunteered a word of advice. "Throw your heart over the bars and your body will follow," he said. In every field of endeavor, those who put their hearts into their work are the real leaders. Romance isn't just identified with the relationship between a man and a woman. It's a very strong factor in living life. Without it we fail. We must be in love with what we are doing. You wouldn't take a girl in your arms and give her a lecture on emotional stimulation! "I love you" or no words at all says it. Approach life each day with the same spontaneity. In other words, fall in love with life!

With these words, the ancient Israelites started a new day: "Rouse yourself, my soul! . . . Let us greet the dawn with song!" (Psalm 57:8 LB). In our day, Norman Vincent Peale asks, "Wouldn't you like to be so exhilarated about life that you can hardly wait to get up in the morning to see what is happening, and then reluctant to go to bed at night for fear you will miss something?"

That's the way a child lives every day. And they aren't all under twelve years of age, either.

Oh—I almost forgot to tell you—that forgotten word is *wonder*.

19

READ, READ, READ

*I read all my life, in dawn hours when everyone else
was asleep, carrying a book bag wherever I went,
a book in hand to every appointment I kept. . . .
Reading books has been the food of my mind, my
memory, my soul, my spirit. . . . Our reading is
where we live and out of it we make our world.*
     —from *Honeycomb* by Adela Rogers St. Johns

I'd like to pass a sobering little truth on to each one of
you: "You will be the same in five years as you are today
except for the people you meet and the books you read."
If in these pages I only encourage you to "search the
scriptures," or to embark upon a reading program of your
own, my book will serve you well.

You are what you read. Or I could strengthen that by
turning it around. If you don't read, you aren't. Maybe a
bit dogmatic, but I firmly believe it.

Don't just read, though. Be choosy. An old adage advises, "Do not read good books, life is too short for that.
Only read the best." And with thousands of new titles
coming off the press every week, it's imperative that you
be highly selective.

And never just read a book. Always study it. Personally, I won't read a book that doesn't belong to me,
because I have found that without markings and notes,
in time, all is forgotten. (Try going back to a book you
read two or three years ago and you'll see what I mean!)
Concentrate as you read. Those times we read from in-

tense curiosity should be the pattern for all of our reading. Think about that.

George Stigler once defined intellectuals as people who spend more money on books than on golf clubs. Ben Franklin advised people to empty their purses into their heads. Anna Peale (Norman's mother) would tell her sons time and again, "You've got to love life. . . . You've got to read everything, study everything, be interested in everything." Are you a student? What you read between trips to the classroom is far more important than what actually goes on during those few minutes with the professor.

Don't lay down a book because it is fiction. The parables of Jesus would come under that category. Fiction can be not only the most effective carrier of a truth, but (because of libel laws) the only way possible to print truth! Nathan the prophet demonstrates the power of fiction in his story which showed King David his sin.

Is reading any book but the Bible a waste of time? The Bible itself endorses the reading of other books when it states in Proverbs (13:20 NBV), "He who walks with wise men will be wise." For that's what good reading is. You are taking a walk with a wise man when you read his book.

Place the Bible at the center where it belongs. And branch out from there into the super-exciting, stimulating world of good, creative reading.

What you read today is very important. You know why? Because it will constitute that first building block for the new you of five years from today.

OUR FATIGUE

20

BUILDING ON SAND

Nothing in this world is free. . . . Good health and fitness must be sought after and worked for. . . . Time and effort must be put into it.
—from *Running for Your Life* by Bill Emmerton

We're probably closer to zero on this "F" than on any other. More of our woes are caused by the "blahs" than we care to admit. And no matter how much else we do to make life more meaningful, if we neglect our bodies, it will, to a greater extent, be in vain. The whole is no more than the sum of its parts.

From the for-what-it's-worth department, here's a thought-provoking definition of the human animal: that being which throws the peanuts to the monkeys while munching on potato chips and drinking pop. Now you tell me who's the fool!

Man is never more juvenile than when he is deciding what he is going to eat. The only criterion appears to be "Does it taste good?" What if we applied this same reasoning to other areas of life—that is, immediate gratification or pleasure automatically makes an activity good for me? (Good food does taste good. But it usually requires a period of adjustment to make the switch. Try going back to cola after six months off the stuff. It will remind you more of medicine than of food!)

We take far better care of our automobiles than we do of our own bodies. We are very careful to burn only the best gasoline, use top grade oil, and change it frequently. Then we proceed to fill our own bodies with junk.

Good health is not a gift. You're going to have to fight for it. And almost any attempt on your part to improve will attract for you, in some circles, the label "extreme." Weight lifter Barry Whitcomb expressed this pretty well by saying, "If you want to excel, you have to be a little eccentric." But then I'd sure like to know who it was that decided who and what is to be classified as "normal." The vague definition I get from society today is someone I don't want to be!

And psychology, over the years, has suffered from an obsession with the abnormal. Man knows so much about disease and so little about health. People who study health and nutrition aren't exactly front-page, though there are signs that this is changing. As I write this, an exaggerated contrast fills my mind. I compare the meager publicity given Dr. J. I. Rodale's lifetime of dedication to helping Americans eat the proper foods and live sensibly, with the infinite parade of newsprint given over to certain "prominent" families. Is the legitimate prophet ever going to be heard above the din of trivia? Only eternity will reveal who this country's real heroes are.

Here are a few of my own unorthodox eating habits. A few of these might provide that little edge that you need to give zest to your day.

Breakfast 1. Whip ⅓ cup of dry powdered skim milk with 2 eggs for a tasty omelet (a good way to get your milk minus calories!). Add wheat germ and you have pancakes.

2. One teaspoon each of safflower and soybean oil along with your fruit juice. (It has to be raw and it won't taste good!) A sensational source of energy.

3. An apple a day. And don't drink it. Sink your teeth into it and enjoy it!

Any time 4. 250 mg. of vitamin C daily. (Double in winter months.)

5. Frequent use of vital natural foods such as honey, molasses, sesame seeds, and wheat germ in cooking.
6. A glass of cranberry juice a day (the Arthur Godfrey special!).
7. Mix 32 oz. of unhomogenized, nonhydrogenated peanut butter (the kind with the oil on top) with 8 oz. of honey. Stir extra well and keep refrigerated. My all-time favorite snack. Eat on bread or graham crackers.
8. 8 oz. of yogurt after supper in the evening, as the last thing you eat during the day. Even if you don't like it, you'll like how your stomach feels in the morning.

Watch out. When you eat proper foods, you don't need nearly as much. If you try to maintain the same volume, you will feel overstuffed and uncomfortable. It takes twice as much of junk foods to get the same nourishment.

And then, just a few lines on exercise. As I said before, it takes work to keep fit. Jogging, walking, and swimming are near-perfect exercises. Make a daily habit of one of these. (I jog four miles a day, six days a week on the average.) Exercise is such beautiful therapy. Helps you get things in perspective. Gets you outside of your stuffy old self.

So many of these eating and exercise adjustments remind me of getting to know Jesus, in a way. Once you establish regular habits, you'll wonder how you ever lived before! It's like I said recently to a college student who cringed at the thought of surrendering certain harmful foods: "Ya got something against feeling good all day?"

21

SODOM'S SIN

The big trouble with Americans is that they insist on overeating. If they would cut down on this matter of eating, a great deal of indigestion, stomach trouble, and diabetes, which are the scourge of modern civilization, would disappear.

—Dr. Charles Mayo

What was the sin of Sodom? The obvious answer is only a partial one. Listen to Ezekiel's commentary on the subject: "Your sister Sodom's sins were pride, and laziness and too much food" (Ezekiel 16:49 LB). And so we follow suit today, committing suicide with knives and forks.

The cruelest jokes (and they always get the loudest laughs!) are the endless party jokes on overeating. A better word is *gluttony.* For people who eat too much are in serious trouble. They do not live as long as others, and they are subject to a parade of related illnesses while they do live.

The Bible associates gluttony with getting drunk. From Proverbs (23:21 NBV): "For the drunkard and the glutton will be poverty-stricken, and [the resulting] drowsiness will clothe a man with rags." Can the glutton afford to point a finger at the alcoholic? Our value system gets a little out of alignment here.

No one is exempt from this temptation, so, so subtle. Second helpings and snacks and coffee breaks soon add up, and we wake up one morning to find that we are in bondage. And that's never any fun, no matter how good the food tastes when we are devouring it.

It helps to consider a few of the "whys" of overeating. Eating can be a substitute for love, the real hunger being a subconscious one which food will never alleviate. Also, we eat because we are bored. And the frustration of it all is that overeating causes more boredom. Sort of a revolving door.

Moderation and fasting are giant steps away from boredom and loneliness. I find that keeping the adventure of each day alive, giving myself to my work and to others, leads me away from the short-term solutions in the refrigerator.

Night eating comes into play here. Any and all food eaten between supper in the evening and breakfast the next morning has no relation whatsoever to bodily needs. This type of eating is compulsive and has to do with psychological hang-ups. I'm not denying that we all have deep psychological needs. I'm only saying that compulsive eating is an inferior and ineffective way to deal with these needs.

You will find the key to unlock tomorrow in the last four or five hours of today. And that key can be spelled out in two simple words—*don't eat*. Physical hunger is one of the greatest of all motivators. So few take advantage of it. A hungry stomach will literally propel you out of bed and into the new day! (The basic meaning of the word *breakfast* is "break the fast." But the trouble with most of us is, we can't honestly call it breakfast because we have been snacking almost constantly since the last meal!)

Today I am thirty pounds lighter than I was three years ago. I have maintained this lower weight for over a year. I discovered that the real frontier, the real "front lines," are found right here—eating at night. Until we face this squarely, we're still running.

The sixteenth-century Venetian nobleman Lodovico Cornaro (given up to die at forty, lived to be nearly a hundred) advised in *The Advantages of a Temperate Life*, "Instead of eating as much as possible, eat as little as possible." This proved to be wisdom far ahead of its time. We must destroy the illusion that more equals better. More food does not necessarily mean more nutrition. A moderate amount of the proper foods just can't be improved upon.

When you stop to think about it, the actual needs of man are very few. Our life-styles are much too complicated. I quote from the *Rubáiyát of Omar Khayyám:*

Here with a Loaf of Bread beneath the Bough,
A Flask of Wine, a Book of Verse—and Thou
Beside me singing in the Wilderness—
And Wilderness is Paradise enow.

22
FASTING, NOT STARVING

A healthy tree needs, in addition to good soil, sun and water, a pruning process. Pruning is not particularly distressing to a tree, but when applied to human experience it can be viewed as a painful thing to be avoided if at all possible. We prefer the familiar, dead branches of past experience, prejudice, and habit, and we fear the removal required for new growth.
—from *Escape from Phoniness* by Aaron J. Ungersma

Fasting for the sake of its curative powers is as old as history. Plutarch, in the first century A.D., said, "Instead of using medicine, fast a day." Mark Twain tells how he achieved a reputation as a doctor. He simply told his ailing friends to do what he did, "fast for forty-eight hours." For him (and many of his friends) the results were remarkable. I noticed a recent article in a national magazine telling of a fasting revival sweeping North America, Europe, and the Soviet Union, with reports that it was an effective treatment for numerous illnesses.

Fasting is not starvation. You are not punishing your body when you fast. You are practicing discipline, and there's a world of difference between the two. The danger most often is not, in fact, that we will be starved, but rather that we will be stuffed to death!

For examples of fasting you need only visit the local zoo, where officials withhold food periodically as a health measure. Show horses and show dogs are not fed every day, the theory being that eating six days a week elicits peak performance. Could this also be true of humans?

It is said that Pythagoras accepted no student unless he first fasted for forty days. If that sounds strange to you, it won't when you try fasting and see what it does to your mind. Or should I say, see what you have been doing to your mind by constant feasting? As John Gardner points out, "It would be easier for us to grasp truth if we weren't so blessedly comfortable. Part of our problem is how to stay awake on a full stomach."

The Bible repeatedly stresses fasting. It is mentioned thirty-five times in twenty-one books. Jesus taught it. So what do we have here? The Good Book lays out for us very specifically a source of great spiritual power. When people take advantage of it, it works. But so often it's the Christian who is passing it up (or even joking about it), and the person outside the church who is putting it into practice and reaping the benefits.

We must first overcome the dread of fasting, and realize that our minds are brainwashed into thinking that eating at regular intervals is pleasant and that fasting is unpleasant. Compare fasting to learning how to swim, or learning to play the piano. At first you are very conscious of exercises, what you are denying yourself in order to practice, and so on. However, to the master, swimming or playing the piano is a pleasure! So with fasting. To try fasting once or twice and then to say, "It doesn't work for me," is like taking three or four piano lessons and saying you can't learn.

One thing I want to make clear—I have nothing against eating. I love to eat! That's part of the idea. If you're not fasting periodically, you've probably forgotten how good food can taste! You have only to try it to prove it for yourself.

Did you know that Mormons fast one day a month? Have we forgotten that as Christians we are involved in a spiritual struggle? Physical weapons just won't get the job done. Could it be that right now you are faced with an impossible problem? A physical need? A financial deficit? A friend who needs God? I've got good news for you. If you haven't tried fasting, you haven't tried everything.

Certainly prayer is answered every day without fasting. But Jesus, when curing the epileptic boy, said, "This kind [of devil] goeth not out but by prayer and fasting" (Matthew 17:21 KJV). Some situations will never be resolved until we resort to fasting.

Fasting is by no means the whole ball game. Fasting isn't the most important part of Christian living—not by a long shot. But it is important. And it is neglected by vast multitudes of God's children today.

23

WHEN, NOT IF

*Those who have eyes only for the sensational may
be disappointed. . . . The value of a fast is not to
be judged by how much there is of the spectacular
or the dramatic, but how much there is of solid
lasting gain for the kingdom of God.*
          —from *God's Chosen Fast* by Arthur Wallis

The greatest sermon ever preached (and incidentally, a
rather short one!) was the Sermon on the Mount. In it,
Jesus said, "When you give alms . . ." When. Not if. And
it follows that serving Jesus touches your pocketbook, or
else you'd have a hard time convincing anyone that anything has really happened to you. Jesus went on to say,
"When you pray . . ." When. Not if. And the word
Christian, today, implies someone who practices prayer.
Then Jesus said, "When you fast . . ." When! Not if!
One, two, three. Giving alms, praying, fasting. Here we
have fasting, not as an optional extra, not for a select
few. Jesus applied fasting to the entire crowd gathered
on the mount that day.

On one occasion, the scribes and Pharisees asked Jesus
why the disciples of John fasted and his didn't. Jesus
explained, "When the bridegroom shall be taken away
from them . . . then shall they fast" (Mark 2:20 KJV).
Guess what? That's today! That time is now. We are now
living in the fasting age for all true followers of the
Master.

Well, why should we fast? Let's do some hopping
through the Bible:

1. To drown spiritual pride.
   The Israelites sang, "I humbled my soul with fasting" (Psalm 35:13 KJV). Two enemies we are constantly struggling with are pride on one hand and indifference on the other. Indifference leads to the sins of the flesh. Pride leads to the sins of the spirit. Fasting helps combat both.

2. To be set free from sin.
   Jehovah said to Isaiah, "Is not this the fast that I have chosen? to loose the bands of wickedness . . . to let the oppressed go free, and . . . break every yoke?" This passage is taken from Isaiah 58 (verse 6, KJV), a classic on the subject.

3. For wisdom.
   "I Daniel . . . turned my face to the Lord God, seeking him by prayer and supplications, with fasting. . . . Gabriel . . . said to me, 'O Daniel, I have now come out to give you wisdom and understanding'" (Daniel 9:1–22 Revised Standard Version).

4. For safety in times of national emergency.
   Reread the book of Esther (preferably with the Apocryphal additions), which tells how all the Jews, including the queen herself, fasted without food or water three days. And God responded.

5. Maybe God wants you to fast.
   "Jesus was led up of the Spirit into the wilderness" (Matthew 4:1 KJV).

Warning: It's so easy to keep truth suspended in the abstract, never integrating it into our daily lives. But faith without works is dead. Or nonexistent. The emphasis of the Bible on this subject is clear-cut. There can be no doubt. Until we begin to practice some form of fasting, we must admit that there are parts of the Bible which we are not willing to accept.

Jesus doesn't call us to just spread information. Our lives are intended to be a demonstration of something miraculous. And without unhurried prayer, serious Bible study, and fasting, the miraculous is going to come up missing.

Daniel had a visit from an angel during a fast. Try to get rid of the notion that fasting is something to be tolerated. It is an exciting physical and spiritual adventure.

Some practical suggestions. Don't talk freely about your fast. (Of course, there are always a few people who must know.) The power lies primarily in the secrecy of it. Also, be sure to spend a part of the fast day reading and meditating on the Bible. This will help offset the danger of fanatical thinking, which fasting on a purely human level can encourage.

A good start is to conduct your fast in line with the Jewish Law. Start after supper (sunset) one evening, don't snack that night, and go right around the clock to the next day at sunset when you break the fast with a light snack. (A large meal immediately following a fast will cause discomfort.) Drink water only. No juices. Drinking fruit juice all day is a fruit feast, not a fast. The idea is to give your entire system a total rest.

You can fast for twenty-four hours with no changes in daily activity. On fasts longer than one day, slow down a little after the first day.

You'll feel better, your food will be tastier, you'll experience new power with God, you might even lose a little weight. But, when it's all wrapped up and delivered, I will never, never be able to *reason* you into fasting. It just isn't reasonable. You'll never simply feel like doing it. Only as God impresses the truth upon your mind and soul will anything ever happen.

But when it does, I am certain that you will see that fasting is not an endurance contest. It is an experience with God.

24
ENEMY NUMBER ONE

*Did I ever tell you what a gift you have for turning
a simple little thing into an adventure? . . . One of
the things the matter with so many is boredom. It
could even be our most deadly enemy. We put up
with all kinds of claptrap and get sold all kinds of
tinsel . . . we grasp at any straw to escape its suffo-
cation.*
　　　　—from *Tell No Man* by Adela Rogers St. Johns

The problem of fatigue stretches far beyond the bounds
of causes that are strictly physical, such as lack of exercise
or improper eating habits. One of the least recognizable
causes of fatigue is boredom. Being bored can literally
wear you out. Someone once suggested that walking ten
blocks with a nagging wife can be more fatiguing than
walking ten miles with an adoring sweetheart (who, incidentally, might also happen to be your wife!).

Billy Graham calls it "the problem that has no name."
I'll call it Enemy Number One. Boredom. Enemy Number
One for Christians, too. Don't kid yourself. The bored
Christians in this country would populate a city!

Proverbs defines a man who gets bored with himself as
a backslider. Boredom is a symptom—a symptom that we
are no longer moving toward God; that we are sliding.
Or possibly just standing still. Like a bicycle. We're standing still with no place to go, wondering why we can't stay
upright! Many times, we have already solved a problem
in one area of life and we need only apply the solution
elsewhere. You can attack boredom in this manner.

One technique is *transplanted enthusiasm*. Think of the long hours of constant challenge and excitement you put into your favorite hobby. Expand this to include your family, your friends, and, yes, even your problems!

No one got bored planning your last family vacation, did they? Far from it. The whole family was wide awake. There was lots of chatter, laughter, and excitement. Analyze the processes involved. First you got the idea of taking the vacation. Then you decided where you would go. Before long, you began to visualize yourself as actually being there, fishing, visiting a national park, or what have you. And finally, the vacation trip became reality.

Could anything be clearer? Apply the same basic steps to life as you live it every day. First, decide to live. This is not as naïve as it sounds. Face the day. Second, fix some goals. Decide what you want to accomplish. Don't scatter your fire. Narrow down to one or a few goals. Third, see yourself doing it. Realization will come, slow but sure, as you repeat these steps each day.

And you can't wait till after breakfast! You've got to start first thing in the morning to pump into yourself some reason for anticipating the day. (In addition to the Bible, I "brainwash" myself with three-by-five cards, on which I have typed brief, thought-provoking messages. I go through hundreds of them in a few months' time.)

It isn't necessary for every day to be easy or even pleasant throughout. (Don't worry, it won't happen anyhow!) But—every single day should be a challenge. And interesting. This level we can achieve. And as we are challenged more, we will be bored less.

When the Chosen People reached the Red Sea they turned to Moses. "Leave us alone," they cried. "Better to work for the Egyptians than die in the wilderness" (Exodus 14:12 JB). Is that your outlook on life, your attitude toward adventure? Do you prefer safety with boredom to a life of danger, opportunity, and excitement? Boredom is your deadliest enemy. Never let yourself become bored.

25

A CLEAR CONSCIENCE

The basic requirement for asking forgiveness in the right way is to concentrate on only that which you have done. To bring someone else in is to shift part of the blame. This is not complete death to pride.
—Bill Gothard

Many Christians carry on their shoulders and in their minds an unnecessary load of unresolved guilt. This is probably the root cause of much irritability and conflicts with other people. Paul wrote in a letter to Timothy that the love springing from a clear conscience was a simple weapon "from which some having swerved have turned aside" (I Timothy 1:6 KJV).

Restitution is a Bible teaching. God required Job's three friends to go back to Job, and there offer their burnt offering to God. When Zaccheus promised to pay back fourfold anyone he had cheated, Jesus proclaimed that salvation had come to that house. And Jesus taught in the Sermon on the Mount, "So, when you are offering your gift at the altar and remember that your brother holds something against you, leave your gift there at the altar and go and become reconciled to your brother; then come, and offer your gift" (Matthew 5:23–24 NBV).

While I was working on this book, in the wee hours of a June morning, it seemed that God spoke and required four things of me.

1. To place a call long-distance to a professional musician whom I had purposely ignored six years before at a concert, and apologize.

2. To publicly request forgiveness of the Sunday morning congregation at my home church for not supporting them as well as I knew I could.
3. To ask forgiveness and pay for magazines I had stolen twenty years before from a school chum.
4. To seek the mind of God concerning three or four close and casual friends, whom I felt had animosity toward me, and toward whom my attitude was wrong.

The time involved in following through on these duties (waiting for Sunday, finding people at home, etc.) was a time of great heaviness. Not depression, but heaviness. Part of this time I spent in fasting. I wanted to be sure it was the voice of God (and not an oversensitive conscience) so I only made one apology a day, and prayed about each one. That is, until the last day, when I made four, because my sleep was beginning to be affected.

This was a crisis, and though very humbling and hard to do, nevertheless very exciting. Anything God asks you to do can't possibly be less. I'll tell you one thing. It was anything but boring!

To be sure of making myself clear, I wrote out each statement of apology. Not word for word—but a general idea. As I approached the actual acts of restitution, I began to have doubts and fears. Crutches helped me here. Calling our minister in advance and asking for time in the service prevented backing out of that. Having specific persons return my phone calls also helped me to stay with it.

As it turned out, I made seven apologies—one in person, five over the telephone, and one by mail (which had been an offense committed in a letter, otherwise I do not recommend using the mail for this). These were all sources of great spiritual blessing to me—and to the other people, too, as far as I could discern. Afterward, I had a feeling of peace about the whole thing, as if it were, at least for the present, a job completed.

The list grew *and* shrunk. The magazine incident faded

(I couldn't remember whether I had given them back or not), and a couple of others were added. It is a good idea to deal with the worst offense first. Otherwise you can cause embarrassment by asking for forgiveness in trivial matters that need no special attention. This can be Satan's counterfeit, or a matter of transferring guilt from its real cause. If you feel pushed, in a hurry, or under bondage, it's likely not the Holy Spirit who is making the suggestion.

This experience, covering about five days, amounted to a new baptism in the Holy Spirit for me. This is difficult for me to write about. It is all so recent. I'm sure my thoughts will be more organized and objective a year from now, but I wanted to share it with you, so here it is. (Already, six months later, I am tempted to touch this up, but I can't. For I want the experience to come through to you exactly as it occurred. Only in its crude form can it be of use to others.)

No one could possibly ever make everything in his life right. But I believe God does require it in certain instances. And in so many ways you're the winner! The feeling of relief when unresolved guilt is eliminated is beyond description. It is also a powerful means of witnessing to someone who needs God.

This could have been the secret of Abraham Lincoln's power—making all his enemies his friends. As far as he was concerned, that is. As I write this, I can think of no one who is not my friend. I have no enemies now. And it was well worth going through what was the most humbling experience of my life.

26
THE THERAPY OF PRAISE

When I was very young I used to wonder why God was so eager to have us praise Him all the time—didn't it seem a lot like merely human vanity? Now I know that like all His commandments, He requires it not for His good—but for ours!
—Louis Evans in *Guideposts* magazine

The Eighth Psalm is a prayer without a petition—just telling God how wonderful he is. That's refreshing. Just to quit begging for more, and thank him for what I've got.

On one occasion, Jesus stopped everything to say, "Do you not remember?" (Mark 8:18 NBV). Five loaves, five thousand—how many baskets left over? Seven loaves, four thousand—how many baskets left over? It is a good habit to remind ourselves of past miracles and blessings. And even to review the details.

Conventionally, we think of praise as following a blessing. But it should precede it as well. Follow the sequence of Psalm 67 (verses 5–6 KJV): "Let the people praise thee, O God; let all the people praise thee. Then shall the earth yield her increase; and God . . . shall bless us."

Jesus even thanked God for the cup. This was the symbol of the extreme suffering he was about to endure. "Under all circumstances give thanks, for such is God's will for you," writes Paul in I Thessalonians 5:18 (NBV). The key, however, is the verse before, verse 17: "Pray unceasingly." In other words, we will be giving thanks under all circumstances if we are taking time for continuing conversation with God.

THE THERAPY OF PRAISE

None of us would ever treat our husbands or wives the way we treat God. Can't you see yourself saying matter-of-factly, "OK, honey, ten minutes. Time's up. See you tomorrow"? You see, when we really get honest, we have to admit that we aren't in love with God. The day we throw our stopwatches away is the day on which God will take on a new dimension for us. And all our days will be flavored with romance.

To me, the morning is the key to the whole prayer and praise thing. How do you spend your mornings? Is it a time of renewal? "Your strength shall be renewed day by day like morning dew" is a promise in the Psalms (110:3 LB). Look for specific things to thank God for in the morning. Your day will be richer for it. That old saying "An hour in the morning is worth two" is still good today. What time do you get up? Could it be a half hour earlier?

Praise helps us to focus on God. And this is so important to mental and spiritual well-being. Verse 5 of Psalm 66 (NBV) is one of my favorite verses. It simply says, "Come and see what God has done." Don't waste my time and yours telling me about the latest scandal, or hashing over the details of the newest "Sinsation." Oh, it's probably true all right. But it's not new. Satan has a hard time being original. But when you talk about what God is doing, there's something that's fresh and real and new every day!

The secret seems to be this constant spirit of praise, which is unfortunately so rare among Christian people. Psalm 119 (verse 164 LB) reads, "I will praise you seven times a day. Psalm 84 (verse 4 JB) goes beyond that: "Happy those who . . . can praise you all day long."

Try a prayer without a petition. And do it today. There is therapy in praise.

27

CALENDAR CAPTIVITY

It was what you were, not how long you'd been it!
—from *The Late Liz* by Elizabeth Burns

When God delivered the Israelites from Egyptian bondage, he chose two men to lead that expedition. One was eighty years old. The other was eighty-three. Moses and Aaron. It seems that today we are preoccupied with youth. You hear clichés like "Youth will lead the way" or "Young people are the most important part of the church." I don't buy it. I just can't picture God being that hung up on how old or young we are. Isn't he just looking for people he can use, whether they be eighteen or eighty?

The youth are important. It's just that they are not more important than older folks, that's all. Psalm 105 calls Aaron the man of God's choice. That's what God thinks of senior citizens. We've got women's lib today; what about senior citizen's lib? I am convinced that we discriminate in this country because of age. No, we don't throw oldsters in jail—we don't beat them over the head. But we ignore them. And some even consider people over sixty-five a problem.

The Mediterranean and Eastern countries' reverence for old age is a joy to observe. This comes from the Bible. The ancient Hebrew Law included this command: "You are to rise up before gray hairs, you are to honor old age" (Leviticus 19:32 JB).

Going back to Moses—coincidentally, the average life expectancy for adults was the same then as it is today. Read it for yourself in the Ninetieth Psalm, attributed to

Moses: three score years and ten. So, you see, the situation is mathematically comparable. What if we had an eighty and eighty-three-year-old president and vice president? I'm afraid that our first reaction betrays our biased thinking on the subject.

Psalm 119 (verse 100 LB) teaches that if we stay close to and meditate upon God's Word, it "will make me even understand more than the aged." The modern man isn't going to be impressed by that statement, because he thinks he already does!

God said to the Israelites, "In your old age I shall be still the same, when your hair is gray I shall still support you" (Isaiah 46:4 JB). When we idolize youth and cast off age, we reveal where our real trust is.

Despite the outward physical changes that the years bring about, there are no age limits for creativity. (I recall seeing the late R. G. Le Tourneau in his eighties, when he had forgotten one of his own children as the result of a stroke, still designing new machinery and reporting to work every morning at his Texas complex.) If we do not neglect our minds, if we do not abuse them, and if we are not sick, brainwork and creative activity go on and on, and do not stop at sixty-five—or even eighty-five. Psalm 92 (verse 14 JB) says that the virtuous are "still bearing fruit in old age, still remaining fresh and green." The two go together. There is a freshness about an older person who continues to bear fruit.

Don't feel sorry for men like these! They have discovered something: that youth is not related to earth orbits, but to a state of growing, learning, changing. All people can be helped to regain the mentality of youth, which says, in essence, "Today is another day. What can be done about it?" And there are some in their twenties and thirties who are already into old age. Thoreau said of these, "None are so old as those who have outlived enthusiasm."

The four lepers at the gate of Samaria speak for senior

citizens today when they say to one another, "Why sit here waiting for death?" (II Kings 7:3 JB). Are you over sixty-five? Do you see yourself as old, tired, over the hill? This is the result of believing what other people tell you about yourself. And maybe it's time to start listening to what God says about old age. In fact, he may be thinking of a pretty important job, and he may be pointing right at *you*, saying, "There's the man, the woman, of *my* choice."

Abraham is the prime example in the Bible of God's blessing on the aged. In Genesis is recorded, "Abraham was now a very old man, and God blessed him in every way" (Genesis 24:1 LB).

And he will do the same for you.

OUR SO-CALLED FREEDOMS

28

TO BREAK THE RULES

Just because nobody tells me that I can't play a saxophone, doesn't necessarily mean I am free to play a saxophone. I must also have the ability.
—Myron Augsberger

We talk a lot about freedom today. Clamence (in the Camus novel *The Fall*) seemingly speaks for all of us in the twentieth century when he says, "On the bridges of Paris I, too, learned that I was afraid of freedom." Clamence recognized no divine rule, no supernatural ethic —and then admitted that this freedom was more than he could handle.

Is sexual restraint synonymous with deprivation to you? Does not being able to eat a dozen chocolate eclairs mean restraint to you? When people ignore the rules concerning food and calories, we get the message real fast. The avoirdupois tells the whole story! What we also need to see is the truth that the man or woman who throws the rules to the wind in the area of sex is just as much out of proportion emotionally and spiritually.

Who would bother to watch a World Series game without absolute, totally unbreakable rules? Or let's try rush hour without traffic laws in your particular city! After a while we begin to see why Christ urged us to keep the commandments, "that my joy might remain in you, and that your joy might be full" (John 15:11 KJV).

One could compare extramarital sex with a football player on the field all alone (no teammates, no opponents, no crowd) scoring "touchdowns." Sex just can't be isolated. It is futile to try to separate the sex act from a complete sharing of all phases of life between two persons.

Afterward, the indulger is immediately aware that he got more than he bargained for. Because sex always involves you emotionally with the other person. You can't just pick it up and lay it down. Especially is this true of the woman. The Bible goes so far as to declare that even when a prostitute is one of the partners, the two are still "one flesh" (I Corinthians 6:15–16 KJV)!

And we need to seriously consider the Bible's viewpoint on sex. (People who don't read the Bible think, mistakenly, that it is Victorian and prudish. Twenty-five years ago, the Bible enjoyed an immunity because it was the Bible, or it might have been banned in Boston because of its frankness!) The Word of God elevates sex and places a sanctity on it. Jehovah, in speaking to the prophet Hosea, uses the same word, *know,* to describe his relationship with his people that is used throughout the Old Testament to denote sexual intercourse.

There is another side to the biblical view. And that has to do with mercy and forgiveness. A fifteen-year-old girl, four months pregnant and unmarried, explained to me in tears that many of her friends said she had ruined her life. Not so. Anyone who believes that lie is very blind to the nature of sin (especially their own!) and the love of God. Jesus endorsed the Seventh Commandment, but he did not make a special case out of it.

I called this distressed young lady's attention to David and Bathsheba, who sought forgiveness from God for their sin. God blessed them with another son, who became a great king in Israel—King Solomon. You will notice in the first chapter of Matthew that these two had the honor to be ancestors of Jesus Christ as well. The point is that we're all sinners, and God's favor is readily available to us in the very moment we turn to him. He doesn't put us on probation like some humans do.

The greatest freedom of all is freedom from slavery to sin. The greatest satisfaction of all is the satisfaction of keeping the rules. Freedom and satisfaction. Exactly what the New Morality promises—and exactly what the New Morality always fails to deliver.

29

TO READ ANYTHING I WANT TO READ

Sex, when harnessed and transmuted, is a driving force capable of lifting men into that higher sphere of thought which enables them to master the sources of worry and petty annoyance which beset their pathway on the lower plane.
          —from *Think and Grow Rich* by Napoleon Hill

The mind is a fantastic machine. Superior to any computer. In fact, it is not even worth comparing the human brain and the best computer produced by man. Some believe that the mind can store as much information as 450 million books! How are we exercising our freedom to put into operation this incredible creation of God?

One way we can use our minds—and there are plenty of customers for this—is to read sex magazines. Did you know that sex magazines are a form of mental torture? They are unnatural. (Here's where we need men's lib! Liberation from this highly sophisticated form of punishment.) Looking at a beautiful woman in this way was meant by God to be the setting for the real thing, not fantasy. Important: I might be able to get you real excited about the smell of food. You might even get high over some exotic smells and tantalizing odors. If. If you had never tasted food!

Of course, any normal man is going to become excited and receive an immediate thrill from paging through pulp. The trouble is, though, it's sort of like saying, "I want my fifteen cents right now, not seventy-five dollars next week!" After a while, you begin to see what you are doing to yourself. Slowly but surely, you are destroying something. You are destroying your capacity for a dynamic, loving relationship with a real, live woman—to whom you are married now, or will be in the future.

God thought of sex. Not man. And God intended sex to be creative. Creative well beyond the obvious intention, that of producing babies. As God works through us, we share in his creative power.

A basic understanding of sublimation is essential here. In essence, this is the ability to switch a desire for physical contact to a similar desire for expression in art, literature, science, selling, or almost anything. This is vital for married persons as well as single, as it in no way interferes with the natural sex relationship, when kept within reasonable bounds of moderation. Highly sexed persons become leaders, if their drive is properly channeled, and not dissipated in pornography, permissive sex, or overindulgence in sex within marriage. Whether you are married or single, sex should be a powerful, creative force in your life.

In looking for help, try not to make a special case out of yourself. This will only cause unnecessary guilt. No one is an angel. All of us have been guilty of sexual aberrations, even the ones who seem most pious. However, God is calling us to higher ground. There is a way out of the morass. There is need for understanding and there is need for motivation.

Our prurient interests are closely tied to the imagination. We all know that pornography is loveless and sick. Yet we find ourselves exposing our minds to filth, and wonder why it causes us to fall. Humanly speaking, when you pit your will against your imagination, the imagination will almost invariably come out on top. And an individual's reaction to pornography is no exception.

I know I'm going to sound like your grandmother, but I'm dead serious (and very concerned) when I say that the only way out is to end exposure to deviant sex in the realm of movies, TV, magazines, and personal contact. This is one place where we don't need to be informed. The apostle Paul said he would rather have us "not even beginners in evil" but "experts in good" (Romans 16:19 Phillips).

Just trying to stop an evil habit isn't enough, because we don't hate sin as we should. We must find a suitable replacement. After Paul writes, "Flee from the lusts of youth," he is quick to add, "Go in pursuit of integrity, faith, love, peace" (II Timothy 2:22 NBV). Lust and sin will come to us on their own. But we will have to pursue integrity, faith, love, peace.

Sex magazines, masturbation, and other forms of misguided energy harden the heart. Sensitivity to people and their needs is dulled. When we give in to lust, God cannot use our loneliness and broken heart to touch others. Or vice versa. For we are running. (Ask yourself: What hurt or frustration am I trying to escape from?)

Sooner or later we must face up to ourselves. It will hurt when we do. But it is the first step on a road to glorious adventure with God.

30

TO PLAY THE JUDGE

*There must be no passing of premature judgment.
Leave that until the Lord comes: he will light up all
that is hidden in the dark and reveal the secret in-
tentions of men's hearts. Then will be the time for
each one to have whatever praise he deserves, from
God!*

—I Corinthians 4:5 (JB)

Playing the judge—probably the most underrated cause of
misery known to man. Certainly the most overlooked
source of unhappiness among Christians. And almost
everyone practices it faithfully. Rare is the individual who
will even concede the need for overcoming it.

Jesus didn't say, "Be careful how you judge," you
know. He said, "Judge not." In fact, while Jesus was here
on earth, he didn't even judge people himself. Though I
am sure he was qualified. "You judge by human standards; I judge no one," he once said (John 8:15 NBV).

Just what is wrong with judging?

In the first place, we simply *aren't qualified.* Remember
the story Jesus told about the tares and the wheat? The
slaves asked their master, " 'Would you like then to have
us go and weed them out?' But he said, 'No, for in gather-
ing up the weeds you might uproot the wheat along
with them' " (Matthew 13:28–29 NBV). Only God is
qualified to distinguish—judge—wheat from weeds. When
we try to do it, we always uproot some wheat that we
thought was weed!

So we might call judging a form of blasphemy, simply by definition—taking God's place. The apostle James records, "There is one Lawgiver and Judge—He who has power to save and to destroy. But who are you to be judging your neighbor?" (James 4:12 NBV). There is really only one judge. Only one. All the rest of us are unqualified imposters.

Secondly, Jesus not only said, "Judge not," but added, "that ye be not judged" (Matthew 7:1 KJV). In the very act of judging, you pass judgment on yourself. As soon as I do it in your presence, you immediately think less of me.

Herman Melville (author of *Moby Dick*) gives himself away to posterity in a letter to Nathaniel Hawthorne, in which he tells his condescending impressions of a young man by the name of Ralph Waldo Emerson, after having heard him lecture. "That ye be not judged" is fulfilled when we pass judgment on another, if not immediately, then years later, as in this case from American history.

The third thing wrong with judging is that it is basically the wrong approach to all of life. I should be looking for what I can *learn* from every person, situation, circumstance. When I play the judge, I cancel my opportunity to learn, to grow. We're all such experts at spotting the weaknesses of other people. If we were half as adept at spotting opportunity, we'd be millionaires!

The men of Ai in pursuing Israel left their own town undefended—a discouraging side to human nature, still with us today. Once in a while each one of us has to confess, "They put me to keeping the vineyards, but my own vineyard have I not kept" (Song of Solomon 1:6 NBV).

Certainly there is such a thing as creative criticism. The editorial page of the newspaper, or even discussion of the weekly sermon, can be creative. But when this talk degenerates to personal assaults and faultfinding, we are tearing down, not building. For faultfinders are fools. Faultfinding never does anything constructive. Often the act of judging itself is more offensive than what we are judging!

What is so futile about all of this is that we don't solve problems by changing other people. We solve problems by changing ourselves. But you say, "I feel like I must be honest." OK. I'll buy that. As long as you promise to be just as honest (vocally!) about your own faults. Is that a deal?

The Bible says that Samuel listened "to all that the people had to say and repeated it in the ears of Yahweh" (I Samuel 8:21 JB). And that leads me to the best advice I have ever received on this subject. It came from one of my teachers during high school days in Spring Arbor, Michigan—Charles Kingsley. He advised, "Wilbert, spend your time talking to God about men—and to men about God. It's talking to men about men that will get you into trouble."

And that pretty well says it.

31

TO CRITICIZE

*Cannot we let people be themselves, and enjoy life
in their own way? You are trying to make that man
another you. One's enough.*
—Ralph Waldo Emerson

This actually happened. A department store executive
overheard one of his salesgirls referring to a customer as
being "in the $1.98 category." The executive just could not
get that remark out of his mind. This led to a research
team being brought in. Later, according to the research
director's careful calculation, it was found that the typical
customer spent $362 per year in the store! From then on,
salesgirls were trained to value customers on an annual
basis, rather than on a single sale.

Criticism. How many times friendships and marriages
are made miserable by criticism! And Emerson is right.
What we're actually doing when we criticize is trying to
reproduce our own likes and dislikes, as well as prejudices
and blind spots!

The feelings that keep people apart are often hard to
detect. It just could be that we're all trying too hard to
sell ourselves to the world. But if we are true Christians,
it is Jesus Christ that we are promoting, not ourselves.
And, if we will do this, others will be inclined to follow
the Master—growing into something uniquely beautiful,
not just another me.

At the very center of this business of trying to change
everybody and make them like we are is the race issue. It's
not easy and it comes slow, but we need to develop the

art of seeing the *man* first and his race second. The Samaritan woman shouted excitedly to her friends (of Jesus), "Come, see a man, which told me . . ." (John 4:29 KJV). She did not say, "Come see a Jew." That's it.

Racism is worldliness in its most subtle form. For Christians are supposed to be people who believe that the *real* man is invisible. What is worldliness if it is not obsession with the visible, the temporary?

Many are deluded into thinking that racial prejudice is some sort of luxury that they can discard when they get around to it—when, in reality, they may be cutting their own throats. Who knows? That same black man you are denying the chance to succeed might, if given the chance, discover the cure for the disease you or some member of your family would otherwise die of!

Let's wake up! We're all so hopelessly dependent on each other. You may think you can get along without the other races, but you can't. Jazz artist Lionel Hampton points out, "It's just like in music—you got to have the white keys as well as the black ones to make harmony." Very good.

I know. It's real "square" to remain silent or to stand up for the absent person or racial group being criticized, instead of joining in—and it takes courage. But when we see racism with all its ugly potential for destruction, we won't want to do less.

One of my favorite Bible characters is Jephthah. His mother was a prostitute. His legitimate half brothers drove him from their home for that reason. But when trouble came to the people of Gilead, Jephthah was sent for to be their leader!

In American textbooks of fifty years ago was found this interesting definition: "Uranium is a white, metallic substance of no known value."

Do you look at certain people and place them in the $1.98 category? Or do you see, over the years, a great potential expenditure for God?

32

TO BUILD WALLS

There is a certain type of Christianity so-called which joins together an unimpeachable orthodoxy and an almost complete lovelessness. It is much more concerned with smelling out heresy than it is with helping human need. It carries with it an atmosphere of permanent disapproval. . . . It claims the right to sit in judgment on the faith and the belief of all others. It may possibly blast men with the truth; it will certainly never warm them with love.
    —from *Daily Celebration* by William Barclay

The founder of an independent fire company said this: "We do not fit into anybody's rule book, and in this punchcard civilization of ours that makes us suspect. We live in a world of carbon copy people."

William James saw coming to America what he called the Hotel Spirit. By this he meant that life would be like living in a grand hotel—luxurious in a material sense, but with all individuality sacrificed, and all choices abandoned to the hotel management. The Hotel Spirit permeates the organized church today.

A lady, who happens to be my mother, once invited six very poor people to church. Obviously poor. They looked the part, is what I am trying to say. The minister, after preaching a gospel sermon, cornered my mother after the service to remind her that this was "a church and not a mission"! Now maybe poor people don't offend you, but it's so easy for the church to deteriorate to the point where all are expected to have similar political views, like

a certain brand of religious music, dress a certain way—
ad infinitum.

And I've got one word for that—*sterile!* For it's our
differences that help us grow. John said to Christ,
"Teacher, we saw someone not in our company, expelling
demons in Your name and we forbade him, because he
was not one of us" (Mark 9:38 NBV). Lord, deliver us
from trying to make everybody conform to our preconceived religious standards!

Slogans such as "Bible-believing," "full-Gospel," etc.,
are hard for me to figure out. Does this imply that the
other guys aren't? "We are searching" or "We are growing" sounds much more sensible to me. No one has a
corner on truth. Jesus himself was very dogmatic. But he
was qualified to be dogmatic. The rest of us are beginners
in that vast infinite world of spiritual reality. I Corinthians
13 teaches that our knowledge of truth is at best fragmen-
tary.

We just don't know where we will find disciples of
Jesus. The fact that Jesus had followers (Joseph of Arima-
thea and Nicodemus) in the Sanhedrin—the group who
voted to execute him—ought to tell us something.

When the Israelites failed to possess the land, some of
them mourned, "Our own brothers have made us lose
heart" (Deuteronomy 1:28 JB). Contrast this with the
example of Barnabas in Acts 9. The Jerusalem church had
decided to shut Saul out because they were afraid of him.
And then follows one of the most beautiful lines in all of
Scripture: "But Barnabas took him in" (Acts 9:27 NBV).
But Barnabas. The name Barnabas means "the encourager"
or "one who encourages." One of my Barnabases was
Johnny Spence. How could I ever forget Johnny Spence,
the ex–pro golfer who always talked about how Jesus had
brought him back from the gates of hell! My brothers and
I were "jes' comin' up"—we were loud, we were flat, but
with tons of zeal! And Johnny Spence couldn't say enough

nice things about the Shorb Brothers. A modern-day Barnabas.

One little guideline here that has been helpful to me—Don't wait until the other guy lives up to your standards of perfection before you encourage him. Try to develop an eye for potential. That same Saul (better known as the apostle Paul) once prayed that God would grant his people "eyes of the heart" (Ephesians 1:18 NBV). There it is.

Let's face it—building walls is nothing more than pride. And one of the worst kinds, at that. And "in" groups aren't what they're cooked up to be, anyhow. There is a facade of intimacy that makes religious cliques look more loving and open with each other than they really are.

Take time to consider these piercing words from our brother James: "My brothers, do not try to combine faith in Jesus Christ . . . with the making of distinctions between classes of people" (James 2:1 JB).

33
TO ACCUMULATE THINGS

Why, Lord, do we strain for golden rings and silver candlesticks when the sun, moon and the galaxies are ours in a smile and a kiss?
— Marcia Schwartz in *Decision* magazine

A Dutchman who had been taken prisoner by the Japanese during the war in Indonesia exclaimed with feeling, "You can't imagine the sense of freedom I had after they had taken from me everything I had!"

Nathaniel Hawthorne's wife, Sophia, wrote in the midst of years of poverty brought on by her husband's scanty income, "Somehow I do not care much, because we are so happy."

Mrs. Norman Vincent Peale tells how on a visit to the island of Bali she and her husband asked various Balinese why they were so happy. The people replied, "We have nothing. It's things and the desire for them that make people unhappy. We like each other." They don't love things. They like each other. An interesting combination.

Media prophet Marshall McLuhan quotes from the Psalms to show the effects of surrounding ourselves with things. Psalm 115 (verse 8 KJV): "They that make them are like unto them; so is every one that trusteth in them." He sees this happening literally in the Western world. Idols have a dulling effect on the senses. Obsession with the automobile causes us to forfeit our sensitivity to our legs, and so on. McLuhan links this to the fact that speech comes to a small child with the development of the power to let go of objects—a pattern he sees being carried over, in reverse, into adulthood.

Today we read lines like "For they preferred a statue of an ox that eats grass, to the glorious presence of God himself" (Psalm 106:19–20 LB) and think, "How absurd—how can the Israelites be so foolish?" But we really don't have to think too hard, do we, to recall the trivial things that you—and I—have preferred this very day to "the glorious presence of God himself"?

Jehovah warns Isaiah, "Shall I not do to Jerusalem and her images as I did to Samaria and her idols?" (Isaiah 10:11 NBV). We Christians like to make a special case out of our idols. But is an idol made out of fiberglass any less heathen than one made out of gold?

And I'm not putting down the rich or placing a premium on poverty. That isn't it at all. This is a matter of the heart, the affections. You don't even have to have money for it to become an idol. It just could be that the have-nots are more idolatrous than the haves! After all, Abraham was extremely rich and at the same time a passionate believer in God. God deals with us as unique individuals, and he laid his hand on Abraham's potential idol in the Isaac affair.

Nevertheless, Jesus cautioned man that possessions can cause him to misinterpret the gospel, and to live a fruitless life: "These have heard the word, but the worries of this world, the lure of riches and all the other passions come in to choke the word, and so it produces nothing" (Mark 4:18–19 JB).

It's interesting that Toffler in *Future Shock* cites the rise in rentalism in our society as a healthy trend, since lives based on *doing* and *being* are more free than lives based on *having*. He goes on to say that the man of the future must be like a broken field runner, for "it is hard to side-step a tackle when loaded down with possessions"!

Isaiah 43:12 (LB) is a verse that stirs me deeply. I have it typed on a flash card, and often repeat it to myself. The

Lord God is speaking to Israel: "Whenever you have thrown away your idols, I have shown you my power." All of us—every single one of us has an idol. That around which our life revolves. It may be good. It may be bad. That isn't the point. If we will just look away from our idol for a moment, we can experience God and his power.

When Ben Franklin was seven years old, he made a mistake that he remembered for seventy years—fell in love with a whistle, became so excited about it that he went into the toyshop, piled all his coppers on the counter, and demanded the whistle, without even asking the price. "I then went home whistling all over the house, much pleased with my whistle," he recalled. But when his older brothers and sisters found out that he had paid far more than he should have paid, they gave him the horselaugh, and, as he put it, "I cried with vexation." "As I grew up," Franklin said, "and observed the actions of men, I thought I met with many, very many who gave too much for the whistle. In short, I conceived that a great part of the miseries of mankind are brought upon them by the false estimate they have made of the value of things."

Elisha's servant Gehazi personifies for all time man's distorted sense of values. After the prophet had refused pay for services rendered, the Bible states that Gehazi set off in pursuit of Naaman (who had been healed of leprosy) to "get something out of him." At the end of the narrative we find Elisha saying to Gehazi, "Now you have taken the money, you can buy gardens with it, and olive groves, sheep and oxen, male and female slaves. But Naaman's leprosy will cling to you . . ." (II Kings 5:20–27 JB).

We all have a whistle. That which we want more than anything else in the whole world. One word of caution: It might be a good idea to ask the price before you buy.

34

TO HAVE FUN

Man's happiness today consists in "having fun."
Having fun lies in the satisfaction of consuming and
"taking in" commodities, sights, food, drinks, ciga-
rettes, people, lectures, books, movies—all are con-
sumed, swallowed. The world is one great object for
our appetite, a big apple, a big bottle, a big breast.
We are the sucklers, the eternally expectant ones,
the hopeful ones—and the eternally disappointed
ones.
—from *The Art of Loving* by Erich Fromm

Man desperately wants to be happy. But he misses the target and just never quite finds the king's highway. Why? Well, there are no fast answers, but—I think primarily we could be confusing *happiness* with *pleasure*. We think that if we surround ourselves with more and more pleasure, this will naturally make us more and more happy, when really the reverse is true. Happy, well-adjusted individuals are the ones who know a whole lot about discipline. For the road to true, lasting happiness often demands the surrendering of pleasure.

Harry Emerson Fosdick once said in a sermon, "Happiness is not mostly pleasure; it is mostly victory." Think back over your life. The memories we all cherish are the times when we were faced with a challenge, struggled, and were victorious—dating a certain special person, the big game, the honor roll. Shouldn't we be on the lookout for adventure and challenge, rather than passing pleasure?

And life with God is the greatest adventure imaginable! But beware. That old propensity to confuse thrills and fun-happiness with deep inward happiness pops up again even here, so that today we have the phenomenon of the excitement-eating Christian ("Follow Jesus—it's a blast!").

Now, if you like to ski, that's fine with me; but we need to make it very clear that following Jesus is not skiing every weekend. Stop for a moment and consider how much of our conservative theology today has hedonistic overtones ("Get saved and get rid of your hangover!"). And then I think of Jesus. All-night sessions in prayer are guaranteed to induce hangovers!

Jesus warns us to count the cost. In other words, it just might cost us something. It might even cause us trouble. But we raise our children to see us for what we are—Christians to the extent that it will not interfere with our plans, or cost us too highly in money, time, or personal sacrifice. Charles Reich in *The Greening of America* strikes close to home when he writes of "adults . . . interested only in the Sunday ball game, the nearest skirt, or the bowling league, as if they were permanent juveniles."

So much of the organized church today sets it highest value on that which entertains. The church will pay the bill to be amused. Whether it's preaching or singing, we must get "blessed" or we aren't interested. (I've quit trying to "wow" audiences. You don't "wow" people into the Kingdom.)

I see this as a subtle form of escape. The problem is that we are just too pleasure-oriented in our concepts of God's presence and blessing. We get a ticklish sensation inside, and we immediately assume that this must be God. But look at Ezekiel. In the same moment that he was being lifted by the Spirit into another world, he was suffering from deep depression!

Remember that Jesus likened the whole thing to doing what he did on the cross—*every day*. The paradox, however, lies in the fact that in this process of dying, we find the life that we had been looking for in so many other places! For a well-integrated Christian today *is* happy. He has fun. He eats, drinks, and enjoys life. But not on the basis of cheap thrills—religious or otherwise.

A black preacher, addressing a large crowd of "street people," put it this way: "Jesus is not just another trip! Following him will cost you your life. That's discipleship, baby. Do you dig it?"

35

TO SOAK IT ALL IN

We all know the person who is really half-watching the clock all the time we are there; the kind of person who implies, if he does not actually say it, that he can give us ten minutes and no more; the kind of person who, all the time, is quite obviously thinking of his next appointment and his next engagement.
—from *Daily Celebration* by William Barclay

When Jacob faced the inevitable reunion with his brother Esau, he first tried to impress him with his success ("Say this to . . . Esau—I . . . have acquired oxen, beasts of burden and flocks and men and women slaves, I send news of this . . . in hope of winning your approval"). But the messengers returned with only more bad news. Then Jacob had an idea. The scripture narrative is lovely: "From what he had with him he chose a gift for his brother Esau" (Genesis 32:4–15 JB). In the act of giving, he succeeded in appeasing his brother.

These words of the Lord Jesus could be your key to turning around 180 degrees this very day. Listen: "There is more happiness in giving than in receiving" (Acts 20:35 JB). The turning point in anyone's life is the day when he makes the switch from grasping to giving.

"I want what I want when I want it," goes a song from a Victor Herbert operetta. Is this your philosophy? "Grab for all you can get" might sell beer, but it makes for loads of trouble in this business of day-to-day living. This is the way humans are without trying. You can coast into this type of personality. But the problem is that, like a blotter, when you soak it all in, you get it all backward!

Much of our grabbing is hidden even from ourselves. We pretend to be so unselfish. Marshall McLuhan, with characteristic insight, contends that history has not been fair to Narcissus. Narcissus fell in love with his own reflection, but he thought it was another person! Would he have done so had he known it was himself? Grabbing can be so subtle. Even wanting to introduce someone to God, to "convert" him, can be a hidden manifestation of pride.

"OK," you say, "I want to give. But give what?" There's a deep-seated fear in all of us that our gifts won't be appreciated. Think of all the gifts floating around the week after Christmas that nobody needs! Year-round gifts can be useless, too. For example, the gift of free advice. That one usually goes on the shelf. Or "something for your own good." And so on. But, believe it or not, you and I hold gifts in our hands that the world is just crying out for.

First off, anyone and everyone can give *love*. Granted, there are countless undesirable traits found in God's creatures. But Jesus didn't ask us to love human nature. He wants us to love human beings.

Give *interest*. Dale Carnegie is quoted as saying, "You can make more friends in two months by becoming interested in other people than you can in two years by trying to get other people interested in you." Practice true recognition, remembering likes and dislikes—even remembering a name can light up a lonely face. But you must really care. Just doing it won't make it happen.

Don't be afraid to be inconvenienced. *Time* is sometimes the hardest gift of all. For this is when we literally "cast our bread upon the waters," as our time is really our bread. Samuel was once so deeply moved by Saul's disobedience that "all night long he cried out to Yahweh."

The very next line reads, "In the morning Samuel went to meet Saul" (I Samuel 15:11–12 JB). A blue-ribbon example of giving, right out of the Old Testament.

And when you give your time, also give your *full attention*. Job pled with his three friends, "Listen closely to what I say, for your thoughtful attention will bring me consolation" (Job 21:1 NBV). People don't need our religious exhortations. They need patient understanding. Job's friends meant well, but they missed a chance to be of help.

Give *sympathy*. Give *words*. Give *deeds*. (Without looking for credit.) And most of all, just *give yourself*. It was said of a certain millionaire, "With all his giving, he never gives himself." On the other hand, a teen-age girl wrote me these lines: "I love the thought behind giving. I could sit all day and make things. I get more pleasure out of giving things that I've made than things that I've bought."

Senator Huey Long once told this story out of an old book his mother had given him. "An army was marching through conquered territory. They came to a big house and told its master they wished to take corn for troops and horses. The master said—'I will show you'—and led them through two beautiful cornfields to one at a distance and they thanked him for his aid and said, 'Now, tell us why, when other fields were so much closer you led us this long journey.' And the master said, 'The first two fields were not mine, they belong to my neighbor.'"

Long then said wistfully, "I wish I could build my life on that story. I hope I can but I don't expect so."

And all of us must reflect that same transparent honesty. An ideal to strive for, but we'll all fall short.

Hopefully, not by much.

*Mankind might be divided between the multitude
who hate to be kept waiting because they get bored
and the happy few who rather like it, because it gives
them time for thought. The latter lead the rest, of
course.*

from *The Art of Thinking* by Ernest Dimnet

If someone drove down the streets of your city or town,
throwing twenty-dollar bills out the window, you would
probably be crying, "Fool!" with everybody else. And
yet, most of us, every day, are tossing over our shoulders
something far, far more valuable—hour upon hour of
precious *time*. The Bible teaches in Proverbs 12:11 (LB),
"Only a fool idles away his time." People waste time—
often without being aware that they are cheating themselves by doing it.

We're almost all born with an inheritance of half a
million—maybe not in actual dollars, but in hours. A half
million hours of life. And certainly that ought to be worth
more than a dollar an hour!

A couple of years before his death my brothers and I
stayed at the home of R. G. Le Tourneau in Longview,
Texas, for three nights. He took us on a tour of the plant,
an inspiring experience. And one statement of his I'll
never, never forget: "You take my money and you have
something I can eventually replace—but rob me of my
time, and it is lost forever."

"Thou shalt not kill time" is not one of the Ten Commandments. But when people talk of how they are going to kill some time, I cringe inwardly at the sound of a very sacrilegious phrase!

Paul's speech on Mars Hill was a masterpiece, no one will deny (Acts 17:22–31). But did you know that all this came about as Paul was waiting in Athens for Silas and Timothy to come over from Berea? How do *we* use the time that all of us accumulate every day waiting?

Is time spent waiting in a doctor's office, waiting in line at the post office, just a matter of staring into empty space? Or is it an opportunity to read a few pages, to get acquainted with someone. You can learn, I can learn, to gather up fragments of time. Or as Dr. Peale puts it, to watch our W-A-I-T.

Once, while waiting for the bank to open, I struck up a conversation with an elderly gentleman who said he was a writer. The man's name was Jerome Davis. I fancied that my new friend was a local senior citizen, and we even arranged for him to mail me one of his books. I was in for a surprise a week later when the book arrived. Jerome Davis had taught for thirteen years at Yale, as well as at Harvard and Dartmouth, and was a world traveler who had conversed with Mahatma Gandhi and numerous other world leaders! That little W-A-I-T produced seven pages of notes for research on the very book you are reading!

Idleness is only the most obvious way to waste time. When we lose sight of the goal, when we become obsessed with mere motion, like so many religious organizations today (the immediate objectives are achieved—filling the pews, new building, etc.—but the basic problems remain unsolved), we are indulging in a subtle form of timewasting. Inefficiency is another time-robber. If the job has to be done over, time has been wasted (though not totally, for you must consider the experience derived).

Oversleeping is a big time-waster for some. Let's try a little mathematics. If you will sleep one hour less a night, you will add three weeks of awake time to your life every year! "What a shame to see a lad who sleeps away his hour of opportunity," reads Proverbs 10:5 (LB). One hour of extra sleep can mean missed opportunity! Looking at it this way should give us that extra zip we need in the morning.

Wasting time, oversleeping, these are actually signs that we feel worthless. That we are not fully aware of our value in God's sight. If you were governor of your state, would you sleep in, or waste time in other ways? Never. Your value, your worth, would be very obvious.

Hey, I'm not promoting feverish activity every moment, all day long. That isn't even reasonable. Sometimes, just doing nothing or sitting quietly can be very creative. Meditation is an art well worth developing. It's hardly worth mentioning here, though, because few of us are meditators. We're just going to seed, and somehow we've got to change gears.

Think of time, not necessarily as time measured, but as time lived. And that brings us to TV. You'll have to lick the TV hassle before you make much progress. The only answer for me was to physically eliminate it. Your answer may be different, but you must face the issue. It's not so much what is wrong with watching TV as it is what TV crowds out. If you can't find anything in life more exciting and more challenging than TV, you've got a problem! TV is the direct foe of reading. For most of us, it is a monstrous destroyer of initiative and creativity.

Nobody in the world has more time than you. The President of the United States is limited to the same twenty-four hours a day.

How are you going to spend your half million?

37
TO BE SOPHISTICATED

Towards the tenth year, things become different. . . .
In a few months, sometimes in a few weeks, you
can notice the change: a little man, a little woman,
grown-up gestures, mannerisms in pronunciation, or
phrasing, a faked interest in certain things or a
studied indifference to others appear; the expression
of the face may not be affected, but it ceases to be
spontaneous.
  —from *The Art of Thinking* by Ernest Dimnet

When Keith Miller's Aunt Nannie died, he said he wanted
to cry but could not because of a lifetime of conditioning
to "be a man." Our preoccupation with social acceptance
and group status is carrying us away from life, not toward
it.

Adults are the most obvious role-players in our world,
but there is a more obscure, harder to detect type of role-
playing prevalent among the younger set—the need to be
"school cool." Some really have it down pat—the semi-
bored look on the face, don't show enthusiasm, or any
other emotion for that matter! And watching a Little
League baseball game can make you want to cry, as one
by one, priceless childhood traits are sacrificed to the god
of "adulthood."

Some time ago UNESCO installed running water,
through a system of pipes, in some Indian villages. But
the villagers were soon requesting that the pipes be re-
moved, because running water eliminated the daily visit

with friends at the communal well. To Western technocratic man, running water is a convenience. To the Indian villagers, taking time to converse with friends was more important. And so we see that "progress" is not always intrinsically good. Sometimes we pay a heavy price for a little convenience.

And that takes us back to the Little League. A gang of kids choosing up and scrapping for all they're worth on a corner lot can be a beautiful thing. But along comes the adult who sees organization as synonymous with progress. And without realizing it he changes a free, creative activity into something stifling and regimented.

After a school assembly, I was rapping with a small group of students. One of them asked which was our most responsive audience. I thought a moment and then said, "Elementary school children. They climb all over you—literally!" She then suggested that possibly the children didn't understand our message as clearly. I wasn't going to let that one pass me by! I shared with her my feelings that it takes a childlike mind to truly comprehend Jesus.

Jesus placed great value on childlike faith. We hear him saying, "I assure you, whoever fails to receive the kingdom of God like a little child, will not enter it at all" (Mark 10:15 NBV), and also "I bless you, Father, Lord of heaven and of earth, for hiding these things from the learned and the clever and revealing them to mere children" (Matthew 11:25 JB). It looks like we have a choice —be "learned and clever," or be childlike and receive the truth.

When an adult is confronted with a problem, he naturally tries to figure it out. And that's a good thing, for sure! But not so a child. A child automatically turns to the supernatural. "Mommy! . . . Daddy! . . . Big Brother! . . ." The adult's preoccupation with trying to figure out Jesus is what's getting in his way. In a sense each one of us must cry, "Mommy! Daddy!" before we'll ever find spiritual life and rest.

Maybe this is what makes Tolkien's *Lord of the Rings* trilogy and his hobbits so popular with the college set. These fascinating books are just full of supernatural happenings. Whenever evil is about to triumph, some great power steps in to rescue Frodo and his companions.

Christians today need a return to a childlike acceptance of the supernatural. We have every right to expect a miracle in our lives each day—God helping us with a problem, providing something we need.

Once when we were conducting a Sunday morning service a young boy raised his hand. I recognized him, and he proceeded to explain how his pet hamster had been lost under the church. Another child followed with a story about one of his pets. This all took up at least six or seven minutes of a worship service! Very odd, to proper adults —but probably not so odd to God, who must smile at our grown-up tendency to divide his world into "spiritual" and "secular," when to a child it's all God's world.

"Let the little children come to me, and do not stop them; for it is to such as these that the kingdom of God belongs" (Luke 18:16 JB). Thus spoke the Christ, the last word for the super-sophisticates. He made himself of no reputation. We humans always want to be "somebody." And it's costing us plenty.

38
TO DO IT MY WAY

People ignore the challenge [to be better persons] because something in them resents being told what to do. They resist what seems to them like the voice of authority. And yet, they are already victims of an authority far more despotic than the advice of a well-meaning counselor. The smoker is the servant of his little white cylinder. . . . The flabby person is imprisoned in his own fat. Again, only the truly disciplined person is truly free.

—from *Sin, Sex, and Self-Control*
by Norman Vincent Peale

For years, man was frustrated in his attempts to fly like a bird—mostly because he thought he had to conquer something. When he gave up and surrendered to the laws of aerodynamics, which were the same in 500 B.C. as they are today, he succeeded.

What kept man from flying for so long is the same thing that keeps a lot of people from enjoying life. They try to figure out how to bring God around to them, when the secret is to adjust oneself to God's way. C. S. Lewis paraphrased Jesus' words in Matthew 24:35 as "Heaven and earth shall move with the times, but my words shall not move with the times." Ditto the abundant life. The formula never changes. All we need do is get into step.

The Bible says of Jesus that he became obedient unto death. Obedience isn't the most popular word around, these days. We all fancy that we are so emancipated and independent. And then we proceed to bow down in humble obedience every day of our lives to our own wants and urges, and the opinions of people who matter to us.

Industrialist Charles Kettering shares this insight: "A problem is not solved in a laboratory. It is solved in some fellow's head, and all the apparatus is to get his head turned around so he can see the thing right." One of the Proverbs states, "Anyone willing to be corrected is on the pathway to life."

You say, "OK, I'm convinced. But what do you mean 'obey'? Obey what? I never hear God's voice!" Think with me for a few moments. Picture yourself standing in the National Art Gallery in Washington, D.C. You are meditating upon a painting—*The Last Supper* by Salvador Dali. Now—allow me to interrupt and ask a question: "Would you trade the painting for Dali himself standing there and talking to you?" You say, "No, because a painting communicates beyond words, beyond the physical presence of the artist. There's nothing Dali in person could say that would compare."

So with God. What are you expecting God to "say"? Are you looking for vocal sounds and structured sentences? God also has his work of art. His creation. Let me be specific. I think of myself on a particular day—the usual number of tensions and hassles. Suddenly I come upon the upturned face of a child. In one sweeping moment, I see myself. I see my day for what it is. And for what it could be. God has spoken. And he knows that a thousand-word dissertation would probably have said less!

Just a bit more on this. Elihu's speech to Job includes these wise words: "For God speaks in different ways; if not heard one way, then He chooses another; in dreams and visions of the night. . . . He opens the ears of men and affirms the warnings directed to them. . . . [Man] is also chastened by pain upon his bed" (Job 33:14–19 NBV). And of course, if we want to hear God speaking to us today, we must apply the seat of our pants to the seat of a chair and read and study the Bible, his message to mankind.

Her name was Peggy. After one of our assembly programs, she said to me, "I used to be an atheist, but now I'm halfway to being a 100 percent believer!" Now that's not exactly the best theology, but this is how I answered her: "Peggy, none of us are 100 percent. We all have our doubts and our hang-ups. But I think you will find the turning point in your life in the area of your *will*. The day comes for all of us (we hope!) when we get tired of 'me' at the center of everything. When that happens, try putting Jesus in the center. I think you will discover something."

They said of Jesus (in the parable of Luke 19), "We will not have this man to reign over us." "Me" being the boss is the root cause of all sin. And compared to God, that's mighty poor leadership!

In Christianity, stripped of its subsequent additions, subtractions, and divisions, Christianity as Jesus taught it, is the cure for all the social ills of humanity.

—Albert Einstein

Our biggest challenge in "selling" the gospel today is getting people to see the importance of it. We're all so busy. There is so much demanding our attention.

And besides, there's such a high premium placed upon busyness these days. If you are busy, if you are active, it is naturally assumed that you are adjusted, happy, successful.

Occasionally I run into acquaintances who haven't seen the Shorb Brothers for some time, and they ask how the group is coming along. Almost nothing I say will satisfy their curiosity until I use the magic word—*busy*. If we're busy, we must be making it!

Just suppose I came back with, "Beautiful, man. Just had a thrilling hour alone with the Bible, isn't that great?" You-changed-the-subject-how-come? is the look I would expect, and probably get.

As long as Satan can keep us busy with endless projects, he has us where he wants us. But once we get real quiet, and take time, lots of time, to think out two basic issues —just two—something is going to happen.

Number one. *We do not see Jesus for who he really is.* We have made a religion out of Jesus. And don't look over your shoulder—we've all done it. If I have a "thing" concerning this whole business of life, it's this: Let's get past all the clutter (and there's plenty of that!), and let's go all the way back to simple Jesus as we find him portrayed in the Bible. Let's discover who he was, what he said, what he did—and especially, what does this mean to me, as I live my life today?

And it's not as easy as you might think. There are religious groups who demand that one go through theological gymnastics in order to know God! But nevertheless, let's try. For instance, Jesus once said, "Ye shall know the truth, and the truth shall make you free" (John 8:32 KJV). Now, you might not be afraid of snakes, or dark corners at night, I don't know. But most of us are afraid of knowing and facing the truth about ourselves. Contrary to the old saying, what we don't know about ourselves usually does hurt us.

Jeremiah's "You can't heal a wound by saying it's not there" (6:14 LB) is a companion truth to this teaching of Jesus. I have a friend whose wife died not long ago. He told me he had tried to get her to go to the doctor, but she had said, "No, I'm afraid I might find out something I don't want to know." And it is ironic that this man is being treated today for the exact same malady his wife died from. "Ye shall know the truth, and the truth shall make you free."

Remember—truth will be truth. And our ignorance, our closed mind, doesn't change a thing.

But you say, "Hey, man. You've got me all wrong. I'm a swinger. I'm already free." Funny you said that, because Jesus received the same response when he made the original statement. Those standing around him said, "Wait a minute, Rabbi. We are not Greek slaves. We are Hebrews. We were born free." To this Jesus replied, "I tell you most solemnly, everyone who commits sin is a slave" (John 8:34 JB).

And that brings us to issue number two. Namely, *we*

do not see sin for what it is and for what it is really doing to us. We give in to resentment, hate, lust, greed, envy, and the like, and think we are getting away with something. But the modern psychologist cries out, "Stop! And realize what you are doing to yourself, emotionally, physically, spiritually." We are bringing upon ourselves heart failure, skin problems, nervous breakdowns—and even simple ailments such as flu and the common cold are no doubt encouraged greatly by our unhealthy emotional habits, which the Bible simply calls sin.

Let's take a fresh look at John 3:16 (KJV): "For God so loved the world, that he gave his only begotten Son, that whosoever believeth in him should not perish . . ." That's the key word—*perish.* I'm not a student of Greek, but I understand that that word is in the middle voice. We don't have a middle voice in English. The middle voice is the subject acting upon itself. With that in mind, let's do John 3:16 again. "For God so loved the world, that he gave his only begotten Son, that whosoever believeth in him, should not *destroy himself,* but have everlasting life."

You can blame it on the preacher, the weather, your parents, the Establishment, the times—but God says you are destroying yourself with sin. We read in the Old Testament that Jonah "found a ship . . . paid the fare and boarded it to go with them to Tarshish, from the presence of the Lord" (Jonah 1:3 NBV). He *thought* he had paid the fare. The real fare was yet to come. The Israelites, in the days of the conquest, contrary to God's direction, subjected the Canaanites to forced labor and did not drive them out. Man still thinks he can tame sin. The Genesis comparison of sin to a serpent is more realistic.

So there they are—the two reasons why a man is not interested in knowing God. He doesn't see Jesus for who he is. He doesn't see sin for what it is. The truth we must face in order to know life is that we are slaves to sin. And the Truth can set us free. Jesus. The very man who spoke the words, "I am the way, the truth, and the life" (John 14:6 KJV).

How do we get to know God? The letter to all Hebrews begins, "At various times in the past and in various ways, God spoke to our ancestors through the prophets; but in our time . . . he has spoken to us through his Son" (Hebrews 1:1–2 JB).

Of course, knowledge of God is never a completed state, but a perpetual and difficult discovery. But first, we must start on the right foundation. And that foundation is Jesus. God's Son.

CONCLUSION
IS THERE LIFE BEFORE DEATH?

The encounter may take place in childhood, as with Samuel, or in full manhood and in the midst of professional activity, as with Peter. Again, it may happen in old age, as with Simeon.
        —from The Seasons of Life by Paul Tournier

Danny Morris, a United Methodist pastor in Florida, tells of his first (and last) camping trip with his family. It rained ten out of the fourteen days! One night, after "blowing" his last match, he recalls sitting staring dejectedly at the still unignited wet wood, his flashlight dangling in his hand. As the light shone upon the wood, a disturbing thought possessed him—he could point that flashlight toward the wood all night long and never, never produce fire.

These are Danny's own words: "I didn't want light. I wanted fire. The church has all the light it needs. What the church needs is fire! Jesus Christ is the fire."

In the Western world today, we have plenty of light. We know. That's not what's missing. What is so desperately needed is a spark—a motivating influence that can come only from God himself.

Man needs not only to be informed about God—he needs to be moved. Christianity is more than a creed. It is a power to be tapped.

I wonder, do we half realize the tremendous power available to us at this very moment? Paul (in his letter to the Ephesians 1:19–20 LB) describes it as "that same mighty power that raised Christ from the dead." Incredible. No matter what your past failures. No matter how hopeless things are right now. The same power that raised Jesus Christ from the dead is being offered. To you.

Forget about those other times when you tried—when it didn't work. God is famous for the second chance, expressed in these lines from Jeremiah 18 (verses 3–6 NBV):

> So I went down to the potter's house, and look, he was doing a piece of work on the wheel. The vessel he was making of the clay was misformed in the hands of the potter. So he remade it into another vessel, as it seemed good to the potter to do. Then the word of the Lord came to me: O house of Israel, cannot I do with you as this potter did? . . . Take notice, just as the clay is in the potter's hand, so are you in My hand.

Don't think of yourself as Jewish, Catholic, or Protestant. God's world isn't built around systems. Fix your mind on God. To do that, you need simply to think of Jesus. Because of Jesus, we now know what God is like. And we can know him like another person.

I leave you with this question from Psalm 34 (verse 12 JB): "Which of you wants to live to the full?"

PAPERBACK READING LIST

Charles L. Allen, *All Things Are Possible Through Prayer* (Fleming H. Revell)

————, *God's Psychiatry* (Fleming H. Revell)

Claude M. Bristol, *The Magic of Believing* (Cornerstone Library)

Dale Carnegie, *How to Develop Self-Confidence and Influence People by Public Speaking* (Pocket Books)

————, *How to Stop Worrying and Start Living* (Pocket Books)

Adelle Davis, *Let's Eat Right to Keep Fit* (New American Library)

Ernest Dimnet, *The Art of Thinking* (Fawcett World Library)

Mack R. Douglas, *How to Make a Habit of Succeeding* (Zondervan)

Bill Emmerton, *Running for Your Life* (Tower Publications)

Viktor E. Frankl, *Man's Search for Meaning* (Pocket Books and Washington Square Press)

Erich Fromm, *The Art of Loving* (Bantam Books)

Napoleon Hill, *Think and Grow Rich* (Fawcett World Library)

Thomas Howard, *Christ the Tiger* (Lippincott)

Charles E. Jones, *Life Is Tremendous* (Tyndale House)

Marshall McLuhan, *Understanding Media* (New American Library)

S. I. McMillen, *None of These Diseases* (Fleming H. Revell)

Maxwell Maltz, *The Magic Power of Self-Image Psychology* (Prentice-Hall)

————, *Psycho-Cybernetics* (Pocket Books)

Keith Miller, *A Second Touch* (Word Books)

Wayne E. Oates, *Confessions of a Workaholic* (Abingdon Press)

Norman Vincent Peale, *Enthusiasm Makes the Difference* (Fawcett World Library)

————, *Sin, Sex, and Self-Control* (Fawcett World Library)

John B. Phillips, *Your God Is Too Small* (Macmillan)

Charles A. Reich, *The Greening of America* (Bantam Books)

Adela Rogers St. Johns, *Honeycomb* (New American Library)

————, *Tell No Man* (New American Library)

Agnes Sanford, *Lost Shepherd* (Logos)

Charlie W. Shedd, *Time for All Things* (Abingdon Press)

Fulton J. Sheen, *Way to Happiness* (Fawcett World Library)

Herbert M. Shelton, *Fasting Can Save Your Life* (National Hygiene)

Alvin Toffler, *Future Shock* (Bantam Books)

Aaron J. Ungersma, *Escape from Phoniness* (Westminster Press)

Arthur Wallis, *God's Chosen Fast* (Christian Literature Crusade)

Peter Wyden, *The Overweight Society* (Pocket Books)

Plus anything by C. S. Lewis
Elisabeth Elliot
Paul Tournier

Paperback Bibles

The Jerusalem Bible (Doubleday)

The Modern Language Bible (Zondervan)

Magazines

Guideposts (monthly), Carmel, New York 10512

Success Unlimited (monthly), 6355 Broadway, Chicago, Illinois 60610